POWER NETWORKING FOR SHY PEOPLE

HOW TO NETWORK LIKE A PRO

RAE A. STONEHOUSE

Live For Excellence Productions

Rae A. Stonehouse
Author & Publishing Consultant

E-book - ISBN: 978-1-9990454-2-5
Paperback - ISBN: 978-1-9990454-3-2

Live For Excellence Productions
1221 Velrose Drive
Kelowna, B.C., Canada
V1X6R7
https://liveforexcellence.com

⧛

❀ Created with Vellum

1. CONNECT WITH US

S ubscribe to our newsletter to receive sage advice and updates
from Rae A. Stonehouse on networking, job searching skills and
other self-help professional development training as they become
available and receive **52 Power Networking Tips: How to Network
Like a Pro**, a free e-book.

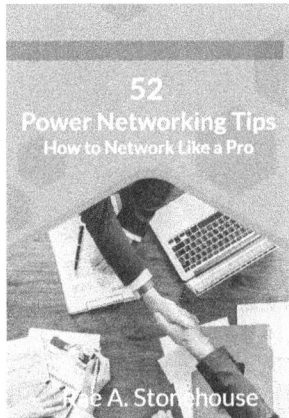

Sign up url BookHip.com/JDGWKZ Visit us on the web at
http:// powernetworkingforshypeople.com

. . .

CHECK OUT OUR **POWERNETWORKING BLOG** @ HTTP://
powernetworkingforshypeople.com for advice to frequently asked
questions.

For even more power networking tips & techniques, join us on **Facebook** https://www.facebook.com/PowerNetworkingNow/

Twitter: https://twitter.com/ powernetworkr

∼

FOREWORD

Wait a minute! Power networking for shy people, isn't that an oxymoron?

How can shy people network at all, let alone power network? Shy people avoid networking events. "No way... no how!"

If this is similar to your first reaction to the topic of this book, I would expect you are shy. Shyness doesn't have to be an obstacle to power networking... if you do it right.

Power Networking for Shy People: How to Network Like a Pro is an updated version of **Power Networking for Shy People: Tips & Techniques for Moving from Shy to Sly!**, an e-book I published in 2014.

Effective networking skills remain essential for business success, especially when we are seeing a decrease in interpersonal communication skills. When I was researching the subject of professional networking skills I expected to find we were becoming more skilled at communicating with each other given the developments in social media and the availability of self-help books like this one however, that wasn't the case. I'll expand upon this a little later.

Since writing and publishing the original book, I have delivered a dozen or so seminars on the subject of power networking to groups of business professionals wanting to maximize their networking skills and to older workers wanting to get back into the workforce after having been out, for an extended period of time.

Both of those groups shared common attributes... there were people who were very shy and there were those who were outgoing. As you would expect, the very shy didn't like having to attend mass gatherings of people and having to network.

Many of the outgoing, admitted that while they weren't shy and didn't have a problem getting out there and promoting themselves, they felt they could benefit from learning strategies to be better networkers.

That's where **power networking** comes in.

I didn't create the term however, I have embraced it and taken it in different directions.

John Jantsch from Duct Tape Marketing says that "networking isn't something you do before work or after work... it is work!"

You don't need to network to be in business but you do if you want to stay in business!

Networking is not a normal and easy activity for many people, especially if you are shy. It is a skill and like any other skill, to become good at it you need to learn how to do it and to practice. In business and in life, a majority of our success comes from talking to people and involving them in our ideas, plans, or projects.

William Feather, American Publisher 1889 - 1981, is often quoted as saying "knowledge is power." I'm not sure how Mr. Feather was at networking but his statement wasn't true then and still isn't. Knowledge is only power when you do something with it.

In this book I build upon the strategies I provided in the original

Power Networking for Shy People: Tips & Techniques for Moving from Shy to Sly!

I will also give more attention to the shyness aspect of networking. Power networking techniques can be great however, if you are crippled by your shyness, then they are of little use to you.

Some people equate being an introvert to being shy. Not all shy people are introverts. Introversion is a description of where you draw your energy from. Introverts draw their energy from within. They often feel drained by being around people. It is an over-sensitivity to stimulation. Shyness is a fear and is a learned behaviour. It is a conditioned response. We weren't born shy. It can be a fear of the judgement of others or even the fear of judging yourself.

We can learn to change our behaviour. I know what it is like to be shy. I know how avoidance and denial can be a good friend. I know how uncomfortable it can be to attend a networking event and not know a single person.

I also got sick and tired of my inhibitions getting in the way of opportunity and decided to do something about it.

In this book I share strategies I have learned in my own journey, to help you gain your power in networking and become an effective networker. If I can do it, you can do it too!

Rae A. Stonehouse Author

INTRODUCTION

Throughout my adult life I have belonged to many organizations. If I felt the organization was worthwhile belonging to, it was worthwhile serving as a leader and soon after joining I sought out leadership opportunities.

Landing a leadership position was not difficult. However, there were two factors that prevented me from achieving everything I could in my leadership roles and taking advantage of the opportunities they provided.

Firstly, I was terrified of public speaking. Effective communication skills are a necessity in serving as a leader and being terrified caused me to avoid public speaking situations. Secondly, I didn't know how to network. Not only did I not know how to network, I found social situations where networking was expected to take place, as being very uncomfortable.

In 1989 I moved my family across Canada from Ontario to the Okanagan Valley of British Columbia, several thousand miles from home. We didn't have any family or friends at our new location. I had said to my wife before moving that I expected it would take us five years to get established. It actually took us more than ten years to get to the point where our new location felt like home.

I believe the biggest obstacle we had in establishing ourselves was both my wife and I were shy, and we didn't have a network in place. We kept our own company and didn't socialize much. We didn't have family close by and we weren't involved with a church, two common sources of connection. Neither did we have a network of friends and colleagues to draw upon when we needed them.

A common source of potential networking opportunities is a person's workplace. I was working in a small group home for the mentally ill. They are not known for having large networks and there were only a couple other staff employed at the worksite.

My wife worked permanent night shift in a senior's healthcare facility. Working night shift easily deprives you of a social life. Add to it the fact of being shy and chances are slim you are going to build a supportive network. We didn't.

Shortly after arriving in the new city I joined an organization called Jaycees. It provided me an opportunity for socializing with the 'guys' and I developed new friendships. There were lots of networking opportunities but being shy I found them to be quite uncomfortable.

Within a few years of joining Jaycees I had reached the threshold of their age restriction and I had to leave the organization. To my good fortune I discovered Toastmasters and joined a club in my town.

Toastmasters opened up a whole new world for me and I incrementally and progressively reduced my fear of public speaking and honed my communication skills. By taking chances, continually raising the bar in accepting challenges and receiving effective feedback from my fellow club members I was able to steadily improve. Nineteen years later I operated a Master of Ceremonies business. I never saw that in my future.

Toastmasters also brought me numerous networking opportunities.

Unfortunately, while my skill at public speaking increased, my skill at networking did not keep pace. It didn't matter how many people I met, I was still uncomfortable in meeting new people in social situations. I suppose I had never been taught how to do so and avoided it.

Toastmasters brought me plenty of opportunities to develop my leadership skills. Leaders require effective communication skills. The more you lead, the more you need to communicate. The more of an effective communicator you are, the more likely leadership opportunities will come your way. All the while this is happening, your self-esteem and self-confidence are improving. It certainly did with me. While I was no longer shy standing before a group of several hundred people and having to deliver presentations, the networking scene still caused me problems.

In 2006 I was elected as the Toastmasters District Governor for British Columbia and became the leader for some 3500 members and 1900 leaders. I had a direct support team of two executive and two more whose roles were to mentor me in my role. All four of them were extroverts and had big plans for me... the introvert.

They thought I should be out there acting as a cheerleader, waving the pompoms and leading the chant of "rah, rah, rah." That's the way they would do it! It definitely wasn't going to happen. Shy people don't draw attention to themselves like that. "No way, no how!"

They also wanted me spending all my time socializing with my fellow members as a leader should be doing. At one point they came up with the brilliant idea of how to solve my shyness. They wanted me to wear a sign saying "Hi, I'm Rae. I'm shy. Please talk to me!" As outgoing extroverts they couldn't imagine the discomfort that I felt.

Their sign idea never came to pass. Nor did I become comfortable at networking while in office.

Over the past few years I have organized and chaired hundreds of meetings with five to ninety people in attendance. This has helped me in developing networking skills. Standing in the front of the room chairing a meeting makes it a lot easier to socialize and network when your task is completed. My default mode is still to be shy and awkward in social settings. I need to consciously work past my inhibitions each and every time. When I have done so, I've been quite successful.

Twenty-five years later and I am still a very active Toastmasters member, learning and developing new skills from the organization and its communication and leadership program.

While Toastmasters provides excellent training and social opportunities, they didn't provide training in **how** to network. Not that I could see.

I decided to do something about it.

I started researching the subject of business networking skills for shy people, likely the same way most people would do... I visited Mr. Google.

Mr. Google had lots of articles, probably millions if I went by the numbers he provided. After reading quite a few articles, certainly not millions though and following up on the resources or additional informational links the articles provided, I saw some interesting patterns emerging.

It would seem most of the articles targeting shy networkers were written by extroverts. Their common advice seemed to be "suck it up buttercup!" I know that expression is becoming a cliche, however their meaning was for introverts to get over being shy and act like them. That is... to be extroverted!

While I was researching and reading articles, I noticed another pattern developing. There didn't seem to be much original thought put into writing the articles. It was as if someone wrote an article on networking and everybody else writing on the same subject merely used the first article as a template.

Writers were producing unoriginal, how-to network articles.

Introduction

In my research I also discovered the concept of **power networking**. I believe my first notice of it was in reference to how to work a room and it was likely directed towards insurance agents or those in the financial industry.

In my power networking seminars I've delivered I would often ask my audience why they didn't like going to business networking events? Assuming they didn't of course. A common response was they didn't like being targeted by aggressive networkers, presumably power networkers. The usual professions cited were financial planners, insurance agents and network marketers.

In an upcoming chapter we identify those type of networkers as being <u>Sharks</u>. Sharks aren't interested in developing meaningful relationships. They only want to go in for the kill. In this case, they want to make a sale on the spot. That's where you come in. You are the target.

Another way of looking at power networking and the way I prefer and promote, is to n<u>etwork with power</u>. Okay, I will admit it seems a little simple and perhaps a matter of semantics.

Power can be used for good or evil. That's why we have villains and super-heroes to keep them in check.

The Sharks are the bad guys. They are using their power to get what they want at our expense.

On the other hand, power networking i.e. **networking with power**, is using a set of skills to make business networking, not only easier and more productive, but setting the stage for win-win outcomes. Both members of a networking interaction should benefit, not only one person as in the situation when dealing with a Shark.

Power networking, at least from my perspective, is acting upon a set of learned skills and knowledge that levels the playing field when it comes to business networking.

This book is written for shy people like me who know they should be out there networking but just don't know how to go about it.

The strategies I share will be of use to shy networkers as well as those that aren't shy at all.

Here is a poem about change I found years ago:

If you always think

The way you have always thought

You will always feel

The way you have always felt

And

If you always feel

The way you have always felt

You will always do

What you have always done

And

If you always do

What you have always done

You will always get

What you have always gotten

If there is no change

There is no change!

Author Unknown

This book is about thinking, doing and making changes. Some of them will challenge you to move out of your comfort zone. Outside your comfort zone is where and when personal growth happens.

As in other books I have written, I use what I call the "onion" method of writing. We will take a close look at one layer at a time until we have a good understanding of our subject. I will revisit some ideas throughout the book, perhaps looking at it from a different angle or context.

After many topics you will see a heading entitled **Power Networking Logistics**. This will be a list of steps or actions you should take to maximize your effectiveness under the specific content area. Each content topic is stand-alone and it isn't necessary to complete the previous one before working on the steps of another.

Rae A. Stonehouse May 2019

PART I

SHYNESS & INTROVERSION

1. SHYNESS OVERVIEW

S hyness Overview:

THIS BOOK FOCUSES ON TWO TOPICS... SHYNESS AND NETWORKING AND how they interrelate.

As I mentioned earlier, I am presuming you are likely shy if you are reading this book. Shyness can be placed on a continuum with being mildly shy, perhaps some occasional apprehension in a social situation, on one end of the continuum and being terrified of social situations on the other. Only you know where you would fall on the continuum. It's your shyness, you own it or perhaps it owns you!

Terrified in
social settings

Mildly shy in
social settings

Shyness is a learned behaviour. We are conditioned to be shy by our circumstances in life. We aren't born shy.

The big pharmaceutical companies would have us believe shyness is an illness i.e. social phobia and they just happen to have a high priced pill to cure you of your illness. You don't cure shyness. It isn't an illness. You can however reduce the impact it has upon your life and the limitations it creates for you.

You also can't generalize the symptoms of shyness. Situations that cause you distress may not bother me at all and vice versa.

In the next chapter we explore how shyness and introversion relate.

∾

2. WHAT ABOUT INTROVERSION?

WHAT ABOUT INTROVERSION?

I ntroversion is closely connected with shyness, interconnected if you will.

Presumably, the opposite to being shy would be to be outgoing.

Introversion and its opposite... extroversion, are often confused or generalized as being the same as shyness and outgoingness [not sure if that's a word?]

However, they're not the same. Whereas, we have identified shyness as being a deficit of social skills, introversion and extroversion are a matter of where you get your energy from, how you recharge yourself.

Introverts prefer to keep to themselves. They would rather read a book or spend time on their computer rather than go to a social outing. Large groups of people tend to drain their energy. Introverts usually enjoy conversations with one other person at a time, rather than speaking to large groups.

Introverts are often self-directed and take on activities for the personal challenge, not necessarily for the attention or accolades. They also spend a lot of time 'in their heads.' Introverts are known to be thinkers.

Extroverts, on the other hand, like the hustle and bustle. They enjoy being with larger groups of people, rather than one-to-one as our introverted friends do. The excitement and the hyper activity help them recharge their energy. Quiet, solitary activity drains them.

As a sometimes shy introvert, given the choice, I would much rather party with an extrovert. Not that I party much anymore...

Let's complicate matters a little. Shy introverts are more common than outgoing introverts. If you are introverted, you were born that way and are likely to stay that way the rest of your life.

Shyness, is learned behaviour and can be unlearned, or more precisely, you can develop social skills which will increase your self-confidence and reduce awkwardness.

It is possible to be extroverted and still be shy. Likely, we are more familiar with the outgoing extroverts that love excitement and can seemingly talk to complete strangers with ease.

I often wonder if the skill to speak with strangers is due to skills they have developed, or lack of inhibition that many shy, introverts display or even a disinhibition in relating to others.

I'm a people-watcher. And since I started researching shyness and introversion I tend to analyze strangers I see in public places and label them as being introverted or extroverted, based on their behaviour.

I have no way of knowing whether my assessments are accurate though as they remain strangers to me.

Recently, I delivered a short seminar entitled "Power Networking for Shy Toastmasters" at a local Toastmasters Conference.

After my presentation I was speaking to one of the audience members who had been serving as our Master of Ceremonies for our conference. I had said to him I was surprised to see him here as I thought he was an outgoing extrovert.

He said it was just the opposite. His default mode is to be shy and introverted. As an example, he said if he was in a room of people he didn't know, he would be the one sitting on the edge of the room, listening to what was going on, but not participating.

When serving as a Master of Ceremonies, he draws from his speaking skills, leadership skills and self-confidence he has gained from being a Toastmaster member. He is an example of a shy, introvert that can act outgoing when needed.

In the next chapter we look at shyness and introversion from a different perspective.

∾

3. EXPLORING SHYNESS & INTROVERSION:

Q uora.com can be a great place to research and to ask questions and receive answers from people knowledgeable on the subjects of the questions asked.

As a way of exploring how shyness and introversion affects people differently, I would like to share some of those questions and my responses. Perhaps they will resonate with you.

If you are interested in learning more about Quora.com, just visit their website. It's free to join and to use. You might consider following me as I provide sage advice in answering questions on several topics. At the time of writing this book, I have answered some 700 questions and have close to three quarters of a million views of my answers.

I'll apologize to you in advance, as my motivation to answer some of the questions was in creating an opportunity to sell copies of my previous book. You may notice it mentioned on several occasions. I've also edited details from the questions and answers for brevity.

∾

QUESTION: HOW DO YOU BECOME CONFIDENT IF YOU ARE A VERY SHY person?

Answer:

You ask a short simple question that requires a complex answer to do it justice.

It's far too easy for people who don't experience being shy and quiet to say 'just stop doing it!'

Life doesn't work in that way.

Being shy and quiet is merely a manifestation of having a deficit of social skills and a lack of self-confidence in the area of socializing.

If you experience severe anxiety over the thought of getting out there and socializing, it would be a different matter.

Being shy and quiet is a temporary state. You can change it.

The first step of course is being open to making changes in your life. Learning to socialize better does require socializing more.

It can be helpful to go to social events with a more outgoing person. They can introduce you to people and you might be able to emulate the skills they possess when it comes to socializing.

Think of improving your social skills as a series of incremental steps. Each step you take should be evaluated and adjusted as needed.

I would suggest creating your own plan for socialization. It could be something as simple as talking to a stranger at the bus stop or while in line at a store.

It could be participating in a 1 to 1 conversation at a networking session when somebody asks you a question. It could work up to your initiating the conversation.

One cure for being quiet, is actually having something to say. It can be helpful to be up-to-date on what is happening in your community or even the larger picture of your country.

As well as speaking or talking about a topic you know about, it can be equally as valuable in being a good listener. Asking questions to a person who is telling you a story can make you a great conversation-alist in the eyes of the story-teller.

Assuming you are over the age of 18, I would be remiss if I didn't mention the value of joining a Toastmasters club in your community. As a member you will help develop your communication skills, which in turn develops your self-confidence. It can be a great way to overcome your quiet, shy ways. It has worked for me.

～

QUESTION: WHY DO PEOPLE WHO COMPLAIN ABOUT A SHY PERSON'S shyness do nothing to facilitate the conversation either?

Answer:

You seem to be making a generalization about all people who are not shy and looking for a justification why one specific person would treat you in a particular way.

Having never met you or the other person, it would be difficult to provide specifics.

Let me address some of your comments.

Re 'I've been called 'shy' and 'timid' but the other person did nothing to help the situation.'

Firstly, there is no obligation on the other person's part to help the situation. Why should they?

Re 'They never ask any basic questions about me'

You seem to be wanting to justify your own shyness. Why does the other person have to ask you the questions? What have you done to move the conversation along? A conversation needs at least two people to move it along. Unless one of them is a mind-reader, both of them have to actually talk to each other.

Re 'or even try but then they label me as the problem but they didn't even try themselves.'

This relationship obviously has importance to you. The fact they have labeled you as the problem and it is hurting you, is evident.

Shy and introverted people often spend a lot of time in their own head. Conversations and re-enacting situations in your head can take on a life of their own. I know, I've been there.

Being shy and timid, which basically are the same thing, will hold you back in life. I would suggest you research how to reduce your shyness and build your self-confidence. This would include developing assertiveness skills as well as communication skills.

Shyness is a temporary state. With a bit of work, you can become a better conversationalist.

Then, if you observe a shy person floundering in conversation, you will be able to help them out of their self-imposed misery. Then you too will be able to say "been there... done that!"

~

QUESTION: I WASN'T ALWAYS AN INTROVERT, BUT RECENTLY (AFTER graduating), opening up to people of all ages at work is being tough for me. What can I do?

Answer:

When you are describing yourself as a newly developed introvert, I'm willing to bet you have always been one.

I would expect what you are referring to as now being an introvert is more likely shyness manifesting itself.

Many people wrongly group introversion and shyness as always being attached. You can be a shy introvert or an outgoing introvert. The shy ones are more common though, which leads to the generalization.

You say you weren't an introvert at school. Once again referring to shyness, I believe attending school had become comfortable for you. You made friends, you were social and you knew what the expectations were of you.

Now you are out in the working world, the rules are different. The workplace isn't going to adapt to you. You have to adapt to it.

You are also in a state of new growth. When you were in school, you likely shared similar challenges as other students did. Now, at work, everybody has different challenges. People work for different reasons. For some it is for the money, others for social opportunities and for others there could be numerous reasons.

I would suggest you start building your interpersonal relationships. Workplace co-workers can develop into satisfying friendships.

I would also suggest starting off slowly. To make friends, you need to be willing to share something about yourself. Start off with befriending a co-worker and see how the relationship develops.

It can be challenging working with people of all ages. It caused me problems early in my working career. As a 19 year old, I was working with some very jaded, cynical people in their 40s, 50s and 60s.

Later, when I started my career as a Registered Nurse, as a young man, I was supervising workers who were more than double my age.

I have also found age shouldn't be a barrier to making friendships. It is more a matter of finding common interests and developing a mutual respect.

Take a chance and try meeting some new people at work you might not have even considered. It can help enrich your life.

∿

QUESTION: IS SHYNESS DIFFERENT FROM SOCIAL ANXIETY?

Answer:

Shyness, encompasses social anxiety and a lack of social skills to use in a given social, situation.

Therefore, social anxiety can and is likely to be an element of shyness.

Both shyness and social anxiety can be placed on a continuum, with low being on one end and high being on the other end.

An individual, can be placed anywhere on the continuum depending on their level of social functioning.

More than likely, a person who is extremely shy will have social anxiety. But conversely, it is possible to have social anxiety and not be shy. Our level of functioning can change on a daily basis depending on our circumstances.

I'm not likely to be very social if I have a pounding headache. Usually I am.

Arguably, social anxiety is not a mental disorder. According to some, it is an artificial label created by Big Pharma to create a market for a product that didn't have a market. The main example is Paxil. It has been marketed as an antidepressant. Somewhere along the way somebody noticed patients taking Paxil were more at ease and were able to speak better in public. Voila! All of a sudden we have a medication that cures social anxiety and helps you become a better speaker. Or so they say...

∿

QUESTION: HOW CAN I GET OVER MY EXTREME FEAR OF TALKING TO new people?

Answer:

Sounds like you are caught up in what's called a 'self-fulfilling prophesy.'

You expect to be afraid of talking to new people, therefore you will act in that way.

First jobs are often identified as opportunities to develop one's social skills, reduce one's shyness and build confidence. As you journey through life, every job you take on from the very first one will add to your skills and experience.

Don't let your current fear prevent you from taking on that first job. FEAR is often defined as False Expectations Appearing Real. They aren't real! We make them that way.

The only way to conquer a fear is to hit it head on and not let it control you.

I've been fearful of many things throughout my life. I was terrified of public speaking. I got tired of being afraid and decided to do something about it. Now I speak regularly and teach others how to speak in public.

Your first job, which sounds like it will be an entry level, customer service one, will present you with challenges to overcome. Just because you are currently afraid, doesn't mean you will continue to be. You may open a whole set of opportunities that could lead to a career path.

You never know what will happen when you conquer a fear. A common response to conquering a fear is in wondering why it was so over-powering in the first place.

Go for it!

~

QUESTION: WHAT ACTIVITIES CAN A SHY PERSON DO TO SOCIALIZE?

Answer:

While socializing on-line seems to becoming the norm, if not at least more acceptable, there is far more value in socializing face-to-face.

If you are looking for opportunities to meet people, check out meet-up.com There may be groups meeting in your area you could easily attend. They have numerous categories that should meet your interests. If not, it isn't overly expensive to start your own interest group and invite people to come and meet you. That can be a good way to overcome shyness i.e. have them come to you instead of you going to them.

Another great idea, assuming you are over the age of 18, is to see if there is a Toastmasters club in your community. By joining, you will have ample opportunities to gain self-confidence, reduce your shyness and have lots of socializing.

~

QUESTION: HOW DID YOU OVERCOME YOUR OWN SHYNESS AND approach people about your business?

Answer:

I'll answer your question in the present tense as working with my own shyness and personal inhibitions on self-promoting, are a daily challenge for me. It is my default mode, so to speak.

Shyness has been a challenge for me throughout my life. Yet at the same time, I likely am involved with more social situations that shyness could be a problem, than most people would encounter.

As a serial entrepreneur, I always have an idea in mind for business.

The downfall has been my inability to get out there and promote my business.

A few years ago I decided to do something about my shyness with business networking and researched the subject of networking. The result was in writing Power Networking for Shy People: Tips & Techniques for Moving from Shy to Sly! In it I outlined a strategic plan for shy business networkers to level the playing field with the so-called extroverted ones.

After I wrote the book, I expanded upon several of the concepts highlighted there such as "blowing your own horn" i.e. self-promotion and using Linkedin as a tool to gain connections as a way to get the message out there about my business. I offer seminars on the subjects in my local market.

I believe many people are shy when it comes to talking about their business and promoting themselves as a solution to someone else's problem.

Shyness is merely a lack of self-confidence and skills to use in a social setting. This can be compounded when promoting a business is factored in. You have to believe your product or service is of value and you are worthy of selling it to someone else.

I also believe part of the solution to reducing one's shyness in promoting a business is in being prepared. Being passionate about your product/service can go a long way in reducing shyness.

As well as having a well-developed 30-second elevator pitch, I believe you need to have multiple lengths of your pitch available to take advantage of any speaking opportunity that may arise.

The more exposure you have to social situations, the likelihood your self-confidence will increase and your shyness will decrease exponentially.

$\sim$

QUESTION: DOES SHYNESS DECLINE AT SOME POINT?

Answer:

Shyness, simply put, is a deficit of social skills. Shyness is not a one-size-fits-all label.

As we go through life our confidence can increase in situations we were previously shy. Self-confidence is incremental. We may not even realize we are improving and become less shy in certain situations.

There is no rule in life that says shyness will decline at some point. It could improve to the point you are no longer shy or at least in most social situations. Or it could actually increase to the point where your shyness becomes crippling.

The differentiating factor is in what you are willing to do about it.

You say you are becoming more comfortable in a specific social situation. The next step is to put those new skills in to practice. Learning more about the people you interact with on a regular basis can help you become more comfortable in engaging them in conversation. Listening can be just as important in social communication as talking can be.

~

QUESTION: AM I AN INTROVERT JUST BECAUSE I'M SHY OR VICE VERSA?

Answer:

You can be a shy extrovert. You can be an outgoing extrovert. You can be a shy introvert. You can be an outgoing introvert, but it isn't common.

Introversion and extroversion can easily be described as 'where you get your energy from.'

Introverts prefer to be alone. Large groups of people tend to drain them. They recharge their batteries when they are allowed time to spend alone, doing what they want, not what somebody else expects of them.

I'm an introvert. I enjoy spending time on the computer doing activities like answering questions on Quora.

Extroverts like the larger groups of people. Lots of action! It recharges their batteries.

Shyness is different. It relates to a lack of social skills and an inability to use them in social interactions. My default mode is a shy, introvert but I have learned to overcome my shyness in many social situations.

Whether you are an introvert or an extrovert, it won't likely change throughout your life.

Shyness can be conquered with persistence and a lot of hard work. Some 47% of North Americans say they are shy. I don't know what part of the world you are from, but I would expect other countries share similar statistics.

If you are interested in doing something about your shyness and you are over the age of 18 you might want to see if there is a Toastmasters club in your community. They have proven to help people overcome shyness.

∼

QUESTION: WHAT DO I DO WHEN PEOPLE THINK YOU'RE SHY AND introverted when you're really not?

Answer:

My first question to you would be 'why worry about it?'

People are going to categorize you one way or another. If by their standards you present as being shy and introverted, that's how they will classify you. If and when your characteristics change, then maybe they will change their personal classification of you.

So what's wrong with being shy and introverted? Besides what some extroverted people have lead themselves to believe to support their own feelings of self-importance, there is nothing wrong with being introverted.

There is nothing inherently wrong with being shy either. However, it can cause a lack of opportunity or at the very least the courage to take advantage of an opportunity and reap the possible rewards of the opportunity.

If you are introverted, you will likely be so for the rest of your life. It is how your brain is hard-wired.

Shyness you can do something about. Assuming you are over the age of 18, I would suggest looking for a Toastmasters club in your community. They can be a great way to overcome shyness. They do so by helping you build your self-confidence through public speaking.

~

QUESTION: WHAT KIND OF SHY AM I?

Answer:

Shyness doesn't come in 'kinds.' It can however, be placed on a continuum. On one end of the continuum you would have a person who is painfully shy in all situations. At the other end of the continuum you would have someone who is moderately shy in social situations. They don't like socializing but they do it anyways. They don't let it control their lives.

Shyness is merely a lack of social skills, which in turn creates tension i.e. stress in the individual.

You describe yourself coming alive when the spotlight is on you i.e.

participating in group discussions where you describe yourself as 'that talkative guy.' Having never met you and likely never to, I would have to ask you are you thinking that this is better than being the 'quiet guy?'

Being talkative isn't necessarily a good thing. To me, it would seem more beneficial to speak when you have something to say. Speak when you can add value to a discussion.

Being talkative can be indicative of being nervous. It can be safe, for some people when speaking in a group. There isn't as much attention put on you as there might be when you are conversing in a 1 to 1 situation.

If the above paragraph doesn't apply to you i.e. you don't experience shyness when speaking in a group, or nervousness, well then good for you! The trick would then be to leverage the skills you use in group discussions and practice them in 1 to 1 conversations. The difference will be that here you will have to listen twice as much as you speak.

Conversation is a two-way process. You have to listen to the other person, process what they say and then respond back to them. Being overly talkative isn't likely to endear yourself to others.

~

QUESTION: HOW DO YOU KNOW IF YOU ARE A SHY EXTROVERT OR A SHY introvert?

Answer:

A simple formula to determine whether you are an introvert or an extrovert is to determine where you get your energy from.

If crowds drain you and you feel refreshed after spending time alone, odds are you are an introvert.

If spending time alone, in solitary activity drives you crazy and you are thinking 'I've got places to go, people to meet, things to do!', you are probably an extrovert.

Both introverts and extroverts can be shy, however it is more common in the introverted.

My question back at you would be 'why does it matter?'

My default mode is a shy, introvert. My Toastmasters experience and other personal growth activities have made me less shy. I do a lot of public speaking and presenting and love the spotlight, but when the spotlight is off me, I go back to my default mode as an introvert.

~

QUESTION: WHAT'S THE DIFFERENCE BETWEEN SHYNESS AND insecurity?

Answer:

It might be better to think of them as being interconnected rather than being different. Interconnected but not interchangeable.

At its root, shyness is a lack of skills to use in a social situation. This lack of skills is compounded by anxiety in many cases. The anxiety itself may have many causative factors. Perhaps a previous social encounter didn't go well. Or somebody hurt your feelings. Or there was a lot of emotion involved, taking anger as an example.

Our mind, works in the background. It processes past experiences, puts its own interpretation on it, then brings it to the present. It treats the present like it has interpreted the past. If you had negative emotions attached to an event, they are likely to be brought forward to the present in the form of insecurity. Insecurity, merely means that a person is unsure of themselves.

So, while insecurity accompanies shyness, can a person be insecure and not shy? While others will agree, I'm going to disagree.

I think the answer lays in how we perceive shyness and one example of its opposite, outgoingness. Just because a person appears to be outgoing, it doesn't necessarily mean they are not shy. Many people compensate for their shortcomings by becoming or appearing what they aren't.

That's a little different from the old adage of 'fake it until you make it.' In one situation, they may appear to be outgoing but if the situation is different, their insecurities will take over and perpetuate the shyness.

Even people that have seemingly overcome their insecurities and become less shy, can still be shy in social situations that they are unprepared for.

∼

QUESTION: CAN I SELF-DIAGNOSE SOCIAL ANXIETY?

Answer:

Sure, why not? You can self-diagnose anything you want.

It doesn't mean you actually have the diagnosis you are self-diagnosing and even if you did... so what?

I don't know what country you are from but over 50% of Americans describe themselves as being shy. The statistics are going up. You would think they would be going down with all this on-line connectedness, but the truth is the opposite.

We have less opportunities these days to interact with people. We don't need to speak with bank tellers or stand in line anymore. We can do all our business at home on our computer or on our smart phone. We don't have to line up anymore. Our smartphones have taken over from where Walkmans started our journey of isolation. Just look at a bus stop and see 20 people with earbuds, turned on and turned out, trying desperately not to make eye contact with a fellow transit rider.

You haven't asked but here is a freebee, if you want to reduce your social phobia, the cure is doing what you are afraid of. You have to start talking to people and interacting.

A Toastmasters club can be a great place to meet people and work on your self-confidence.

~

QUESTION: WILL CHANGING MY SHY ANXIOUS PERSONALITY MAKE ME inauthentic?

Answer:

Short answer to your question... yes, it most likely would, if the change you are referring to is only a cosmetic change to your personality i.e. a cover-up.

Now, I will expand upon on how to avoid being inauthentic if you do change your shy, anxious personality.

I would like to start off my addressing your 'shy, anxious personality.' Merriam-Webster defines personality as 'the set of emotional qualities, ways of behaving, etc., that makes a person different from other people; attractive qualities (such as energy, friendliness, and humour) that make a person interesting or pleasant to be with; attractive qualities that make something unusual or interesting.'

Do you notice that it doesn't say anything about being born with a certain personality and you have it for the rest of your life?

Being shy and anxious are symptoms of experiencing fear. Shyness is related to being uncomfortable or fearful in social situations due to not having the social skills to utilize.

Anxiety may be related to the shyness experienced in social situations, or it may be a symptom on its own. Shyness can produce anxiety in social situations. Then again, anxiety can produce shyness in social situations. Anxiety can occur at other times or seemingly not related to any identifiable cause.

You make comments about the 'suggested techniques to talk and gain confidence' being just rehearsed actions that aren't the real you. It's hard to comment not having seen the advice you are referring to.

It can be argued everything we do in life is a series of 'rehearsed' actions.

Assuming the techniques suggested to you have value, I'm wondering how often and for how long you've actually tried them?

It has been said that a person needs to use the changed behaviour for some 21 to 28 days before a habit is broken and the new behaviour becomes the norm.

I recall a saying years ago from Tony Robbins, who said something to the effect of "you aren't going to change your ways to new ways until you reach the point that staying the same is worse than making the changes."

Your personality isn't static. It is dynamic, meaning every life experience you have, every new lesson, whether good or bad, changes your personality. We are ever evolving.

You are worried about being inauthentic. That would only happen if you let it. If you take progressive steps to develop your personality, your values and beliefs will also change. As you become more comfortable with yourself, your authenticity will likely increase rather than decrease as you fear.

I'm not going to recommend topics or exercises for you, as that is the subject for another post.

~

QUESTION: HOW AM I SUPPOSED TO NETWORK IF I AM SHY AND socially anxious and avoid social events?

Answer:

Well, the good news, if there is any, is you are not alone. I don't know where in the world you are located but the Shyness Institute, located in the USA, reports that more than 50% of North Americans describe themselves as being shy in social situations.

You would think with all this social media and on-line connectedness, we would be becoming more social and less shy, but the opposite is true. This collective increase in our shyness has been attributed to several causes.

Going back to the 1950s, the invention of TV dinners may have been the start of it. Families were no longer sitting together for their evening meals and sharing the events of their day. Conversational skills started to decline. As the years and decades have passed, there has been a further erosion in families spending quality time together in what was considered a traditional family dinner. Families nowadays come in all different styles and there really isn't anything traditional at all. Many children have been deprived of opportunity to develop their conversational skills historically provided at shared family meals.

Along comes the invention of the Sony Walkman. We were able to listen to our tunes on our earphones and didn't have to listen to anyone else. ATM (automatic teller machines) have been considered another step in the increase of our shyness. We no longer have to stand in line to do our banking. That means we no longer talk to other people in the line or the teller. The same applies to many stores. We use self-checkout and don't have to have social conversation anymore, if we choose not to.

Technology developed from Walkmans to Discmans and now to smartphones that can store a phenomenal amount of music. One only has to look at a bus stop to see a dozen or so people intently looking at their smart phones, earbuds in place, frantically trying to avoid making eye contact with anyone else. It's sad, but it seems to be our new reality. If we let it!

The thing about shyness is that we all experience it differently. Simply put, shyness is a lack of self-confidence and skills to use in a social situation. Nothing more... nothing less. It doesn't mean you are a bad person or a loser. It just means you haven't yet developed your skills in this area.

Unless one experiences shyness themself, I don't think they can truly appreciate how debilitating it can be. I think the advice of 'suck it up buttercup' is worthless and insensitive.

Many people have conquered shyness and you can too. It will take a lot of work though. I have been fighting it all my life. I consider it a life-long journey of conquering shyness. I've researched shyness, I've studied it, I've written about it and I speak about it. Some days I am fearless, some days my shyness will get the better of me and I will avoid attending an event.

I too have challenges with shyness preventing me from being effective in business networking. Networking is something you have to do if you want to stay in business. I've heard it said, that if you are not networking... you are not working! I believe that to be true. And you also have to be networking all the time.

As part of my own self-directed cure for shyness and self-confidence in business networking I researched and wrote a book entitled Power Networking for Shy People: Tips & Techniques for moving from Shy to Sly!

Throughout the book I provided a series of strategies to level the playing field for shy people, helping them become effective network-ers. I believe you can still be shy and be an effective networker. I believe the quality of the networking encounters is more important than the quantity as some would have you believe.

Conquering a fear of any subject, with mastery of the subject in mind, is merely a matter of taking a series of small steps towards the goal. Having a plan in writing, with a series of steps leading towards achieving the goal, is even better.

∼

IN OUR NEXT CHAPTER WE LOOK AT **POWER NETWORKING**.

4. POWER NETWORKING OVERVIEW

P ower Networking Overview

Some people seem to enjoy networking so much. They look like they are having fun. I wonder though... are they really <u>socializing</u> rather than <u>actually</u> networking? I would expect they are extroverts. Being an extrovert doesn't necessarily make them a good networker.

Networking is an acquired skill developed from training, practice and experience. Are they gaining benefit from and providing value to the people they talk with or are they just having a good time talking to old and new friends?

A lot of people spend time <u>networking</u> but not so much on **how** to network. Only a small percentage actually study <u>how to</u> network. Learning how to network opens you up to possibilities.

To be successful in networking you need to develop the right mind and skill set. While you are thinking about becoming a better networker, you also need to think about <u>why</u> you are networking in the first place.

Expanding your network increases the possibility for referrals and business to come your way. It is important to teach your connections what would make a good referral for you and don't forget to ask for the referral!

We'll look at asking for referrals later on.

$\sim$

In the first version of this book I identified three phases to a networking opportunity:

- **Pre-networking Phase**
- **Live Face to Face Networking Phase**
- **Post Networking Phase**

As these three phases form the basis for the system I have created to level the playing field for us shy, introverts with the extroverts of the business world, we'll take another look at the steps and strategies involved.

While we proceed through this book we will peel back layers of our onion and take an in depth look at each of these phases.

Before we explore the three phases though, let's look at what networking is and what it isn't.

PART II

THE THREE PHASES OF NETWORKING

5. NETWORKING IS...

- Networking is 'do onto others.'
- Networking is going the extra mile, taking the next step.
- Networking is an attitude, an approach to life.
- Networking consists of gathering, collecting and distributing information.
- Networking is promoting, empowering, supporting, nurturing, connecting and relating to other people.
- Networking is a communication process, exchanging information & receiving advice & referrals.
- Networking is creating relationships whereby you can help others achieve their goals, which in turn will help you achieve yours.
- Networking is people connecting with people, linking ideas & resources.
- Networking is communication that creates the linkage between people & clusters of people.
- Networking is establishing connections that are mutually satisfying, helpful & uplifting.
- Networking is about results & relationships, effectiveness & efficiency, graciousness & persistence.

- Networking is efficient because we use the skills, strengths & expertise of others.
- Networking shouldn't be about selling, it should be about seeking common ground or opportunities.

On the other hand...

$\sim$

6. NETWORKING ISN'T...

- Networking is not prospecting.
- Networking is not selling.
- Networking is not about getting someone else to say or do what you want.

N etworking has been around forever and always will be. Networking leads to new relationships, new opportunities and greater accomplishments.

Power Networking means the power that comes from a spirit of giving and sharing.

To be **powerful as a networker** you must acknowledge and appreciate the power of networking and your own power as a networker.

As a **power networker** you should look for opportunities to contribute your ideas.

~

7. PRE NETWORKING PHASE

P re-Networking Phase

The first stage of my power networking strategy is the **Pre-Networking Phase**. These are tasks and activities you can undertake in advance of a face-to-face meeting with another networker.

These strategies help build your networking skills and your self-confidence.

Overview: (we expand upon all of these items in the upcoming chapters)

Who are you?

- Personal Branding
- What do you stand for?
- What is your USP?
- Introduction to your network web

Are you Linkedin? (We explore this content in Section III)

- Your personal marketing agency
- Your personal research department

- Blow your own horn!
- Reach out and Link somebody
- Send messages out to your connections
- Create a database of connections
- Participate in Groups

HOW HIGH DOES YOUR ELEVATOR GO?

- 30 seconds? 60 seconds... 10 minutes?
- Different buildings?

IT'S ALL ABOUT YOU!

- Questions you will answer
- Questions you won't answer
- Your Questions Toolbox

Technology Revisited

- Your e-mail signature file
- Your personal domain name

❧

8. PERSONAL BRANDING

K nock knock! Who's there? Rae. Rae who? Exactly...
Rae who!

Having low esteem for many years I had challenges in defining, at least to myself, who I actually was. Traditionally, men tend to introduce themselves in relation to what they do for a living. "Hello, I'm Rae Stonehouse and I'm a Registered Nurse having worked in mental health for over 40 years."

Women, conversely, tend to introduce themselves in relation to their role in life. "I'm Diane and I am the mother of energetic four year old twin boys, my husband is a doctor and... oh... I'm also a nurse."

As I took on more volunteer roles and developed entrepreneurial ventures, my identity became a little complicated. In addition to being a nurse I was also a former Boy Scout Leader; a Toastmasters member and a leader; Chairman of a local non-profit agency to support entrepreneurs; a business owner developing an event planning business; a master of ceremonies; a wedding reception emcee and an independent legal services broker. Whew! I'm overwhelmed just writing it down.

Can you imagine what it would be like to be on the receiving end of my introductions? It would take ten minutes or so for me to recite and describe all of my roles and it often did.

It didn't work for me. It often left my listener overwhelmed and confused. It likely appeared that I lacked focus. And at times I certainly did.

While I was likely at the far end of the continuum as to depth of identity, take the following as an example of someone on the other end of the identity continuum.

A young woman goes to university and obtains her degree in a specialized field. She works for a few years and becomes proficient in her field. She decides to marry and raise a family. She leaves the workforce to care for her children.

Ten years later the children are in school throughout the day and she is ready to go back to work. The problem is while she was working, her identity was tied into her job. Having been a full time mother for the last ten years, it has become her new identity.

She finds she likely wouldn't be able to perform in a job similar to her former one because there have been incredible changes in her field and she hasn't kept up with them.

So what is her identity? She still has her degree and always will but would be unable to work in a similar job without taking significant educational and training upgrading. She is still a mother but that doesn't help much on her resume. She faces an identity crisis.

A few years ago I read a book by William Bridges... **Creating You & Company: Learn to think like the CEO of your own company**. He encourages you to market yourself as if you are the company. Blow your own horn! If you don't, who will?

Reading the book helped provide clarity and peace of mind for me. Rather than being a person with multiple personalities it was more like having multiple personas. I have worked in mental health for many years and have met a few multiple personalities. They are good people!

I was able to redefine myself in a new way. "Hello, I'm Rae Stone-house. I am a writer, author, speaker and a self-publisher. My business is Live For Excellence Productions and I help writers become paid authors."

I'll leave it as that at for my understanding of who I am. I have an elevator pitch for each of those personas mentioned earlier, that I use in specific situations. I will describe them in further depth later in an upcoming chapter.

This chapter's content is excerpted from another book I have under development entitled **Blow Your Own Horn: Marketing & Promotional Strategies for Business Professionals.**

∼

Branding

Let's start off by determining what a brand is.

From Wikipedia...

A brand is a name, term, design, symbol, or other feature that distinguishes one seller's product from those of others.

Brands are used in business, marketing and advertising.

A brand is any name, design, style, words or symbols used singularly or in combination that distinguish one product from another in the eyes of the customer.

Branding is a set of marketing and communication methods that help to distinguish a company from competitors and create a lasting impression in the minds of customers.

The key components that form a brand's toolbox include a brand's identity, brand communication (such as by logos and trademarks), brand awareness, brand loyalty and various brand management strategies.

We are all familiar with commercial branding and are likely bombarded with it everyday. Coca Cola, Pepsi Cola and Nike readily come to mind.

These are well established brands.

Personal Branding Defined

Again, according to Wikipedia, personal branding is the practice of people marketing themselves and their careers as brands.

Let's expand upon the concept of Personal Branding.

While previous self-help management techniques were about self-improvement, the personal-branding concept suggests instead that success comes from self-packaging.

The term is thought to have been first used and discussed in a 1997 article by Tom Peters.

Personal branding is essentially the ongoing process of establishing a prescribed image or impression in the mind of others about an individual, group, or organization.

Personal branding often involves the application of one's name to various products.

Athletes and celebrities come to mind.

If that is your situation, well good for you!

I would expect that you have staff to look after you.

For the rest of us mere mortals, let's drill down a little.

So why don't we self-promote?

There are likely numerous reasons many of us don't like to talk about ourselves to others.

Many of us have likely been taught at a young age from our mothers that it is wrong to promote yourself.

"It is bragging and nobody likes braggarts!"

That may be a generalization and it really isn't fair to pick on mothers, considering all the good they do for us.

However, while many people likely don't like braggarts, it doesn't necessarily follow that talking about yourself in a favourable light... is bragging.

Walt Whitman was an American Cowboy poet, essayist and journalist, way back in the mid to late 1800s.

I'm fond of his quote about personal branding.

He probably didn't relate it any way to personal branding but here goes...

"If you done it... it ain't bragging!"

I think Walt hit the proverbial nail on the head. If you have done something and you talk about it, then it isn't bragging.

That sounds like self-promotion to me.

Can you think of any other reasons that we don't self-promote?

It could be a simple matter of we really don't know how to promote ourselves.

Through this chapter and upcoming chapters I'm hoping the strategies I provide will help resolve the problem if you identify with not knowing how to promote yourself.

As your skill in self-promotion increases and your self-confidence as well, you should find it easier to self-promote.

Another simple reason may be we don't have time to self-promote.

Then there is a simple reason that most of us have likely experienced at one time or another. It can be embarrassing at first when you create promotional copy, featuring yourself in a good light.

If you've written a resume lately, that's exactly what you had to do.

In an upcoming chapter we focus on on-line reputation management.

One of the features of social media platforms is that they often require you to create a Bio or a Profile as a term of your membership.

While these can be a great opportunity for self-promotion, the first few times can be challenging.

Do you write your promotional copy in the first person as "I did this, this and this..."

Or do you write it in the 3rd person, "Rae Stonehouse, renowned best selling author is known for..."

Okay, so I'm not a best selling author yet, but I have a head-start on promoting it.

Before we move on to the next chapter, if you haven't done it recently, Google your name and see what comes up.

It is always a good idea to research yourself, just in case you have to do some damage control.

So... how do we self-promote?

((⚡)) Power Networking Logistics

1. Answer the question... "Who am I?"
2. Develop a personal brand. What do you want the public to know about you?
3. Google your name.

9. WHAT DO YOU STAND FOR?

I f you were asked to describe yourself in one word or perhaps a few, what would they be? If I were to ask a colleague or friend of yours the same question, would they offer the same words as yours?

If I were asked that question 10 to 15 years back I would say I was a catalyst. As a nurse therapist I helped my patients and fellow staff to move forward with problems in their lives that were holding them back.

I no longer serve in that manner in my job so I don't believe the word catalyst fits me anymore. Now the words creative, systematic, organized, loyal and persistent come to mind.

What word would you use to describe yourself?

Recently, I learned of an acronym that resonates with me. **H.O.P.E.**

Helping Other People Evolve. I may not be doing so in my nursing job right now but I certainly am a catalyst in the self-help books I write and publish and the systems and strategies I create. The words I used to describe myself ring true and serve me in helping others evolve.

So what words would you use to describe yourself? Do you walk your talk? Do others know what you stand for? Have you told them? Maybe you should. That's all part of the blowing your own horn concept. People aren't mind readers. Sometimes you have to tell them what they should be thinking. That's called marketing. It would also likely be a good idea to ask the people in your life what they believe you stand for. That's called research. Their answer may surprise you.

I will likely remember for the rest of my days, one example of a person who did not walk their talk. He was the keynote motivational speaker at a conference I attended and was promoting healthy living, being everything that you could be and leading by example. I observed him later that evening in the hotel's bar, pounding back the liquor and smoking like a chimney.

I think the message here is when you are developing your professional image you need to have it turned on at all times. In small communities, people you network with in business situations will likely encounter you at social get-togethers or at the grocery store.

Power Networking Logistics

1. What words would you use to describe yourself?
2. Answer the question... "What do I stand for?"
3. Ask friends and colleagues in your existing network what words they would use to describe you.
4. Ask your friends and colleagues if they believe you 'walk your talk.'
5. If they reply "No, you don't", what will you now do with this information?

10. YOUR USP

Your unique selling proposition (a.k.a. **unique selling point,** universal selling point or **USP**) is a marketing concept used to differentiate yourself from your competitors or others in the market place.

Some good recent examples of products with a clear USP are:

- Head & Shoulders "You get rid of dandruff"

Some unique propositions that were pioneers when they were introduced:

- Dominoes Pizza : "You get fresh, hot pizza delivered to your door in 30 minutes or less--or it's free."
- Fed Ex: "When your package absolutely, positively has to get there overnight"
- M&Ms: "Melts in your mouth, not in your hand"
- Metropolitan Life: "Get Met, It Pays"

The term USP has been largely replaced by the concept of a **Positioning Statement.**

Positioning is determining what place a brand (tangible good or service) should occupy in the consumer's mind in comparison to its competition. A position is often described as the meaningful difference between the brand and its competitors. **Source:** Wikipedia

I recently was blindsided at a Chamber of Commerce function in my city when we were standing in circle participating in what they call a power networking session. We were asked what makes us or our business unique. I didn't recognize it as a USP question and provided an ineffective response. If I had recognized it for what it was i.e. a USP question I would have responded with "Mr. Emcee is a full service event organizer. From start to finish... we do it all!"

Your challenge is to develop a USP that on one hand is short and to the point, yet is clear enough that it captures the essence of your business and will stick in the mind of whoever you are sharing it with. Having it prepared in advance, believing in it and being able to recite it with a moment's notice will go a long way in reducing your anxiety and fear which are all part of shyness.

I would also suggest researching your competitors or others that are in a similar business that are not necessarily your competitors to see if they have chosen a similar USP as you have. I am aware of two business coaches who chose a USP that had only one word that was different.

That one word totally changed the context of the USP but it really upset one of the coaches accusing the other of stealing her idea, even though they had been developed independent of each other.

Power Networking Logistics

1. Research your competitors to learn what their USPs are.
2. Create a USP for your business.
3. Share it with colleagues and ask their opinion. Ask if it makes sense. Ask if it is easy to understand. Ask if it captures the essence of your business.
4. Try using it a few times in networking sessions and see what feedback that you get.
5. Once you are comfortable with your USP incorporate it into all of your marketing material i.e. business cards, website, voice mail, e-mail signature file.

$\sim$

11. INTRODUCTION TO YOUR NETWORK WEB

The next three chapters are excerpted from my book **You're Hired! Job Search Strategies That Work.**

While you may not be currently looking for work, I have left the job-searching references within the text as I believe they are relevant to understanding how networking works.

Networking has been identified by those in the job-searching profession as being one of the most effective activities you can do to find a job. And as I mentioned above, you may not be currently looking for work, however there is uncertainty in the workplace. Just because you have a comfortable job right now, there is no guarantee it will continue. Networking can open up opportunities for you. Perhaps a new job or even a new career can result.

~

INTRODUCTION TO YOUR NETWORK WEB

IN THIS CHAPTER, WE LOOK AT HOW TO CREATE AND USE YOUR NETWORK Web to help search for your job.

We will also look at strategies to help you when you are out there networking. I call them power networking strategies.

But before we do so, it is probably a good idea to explain what a Network Web is and why you should create one.

In the not too distant past there was a principal identified as Six Degrees of Separation.

According to Wikipedia... Six degrees of separation is the idea all living things and everything else in the world are six or fewer steps away from each other so a chain of 'a friend of a friend' statements can be made to connect any two people in a maximum of six steps.

It was originally set out by Frigyes Karinthy in 1929. Karinthy was apparently a Hungarian Author.

With the rapid development of on-line social media venues, it has been said the degrees of separation that connect you to almost anybody in the world is now down to three degrees.

So how do we take advantage of this worldwide interconnectedness?

The answer to that question while it is an easy one, does take some work.

The **Network Web** is a tool that helps you draw upon your personal network to find the ideal job you are looking for. Your ideal job may not be posted yet, in fact, it may not even be created yet. Your Network Web can help put you in front of decision makers and key people that are in the position to hire you.

STEP ONE IS TO MAKE A LIST OF YOUR PERSONAL CATEGORIES.

These are your interests and the organizations, formal and informal you belong to.

These may include hobbies, family, church, professional organizations, sports teams, current and past employment.

Create a page for each of the above categories as well as any others you can think of.

Once you have completed the task, please go to the next step in this strategy.

Step Two is to make a list of people you know in each category, start with a list of 10 names for each organization or interest category and then add 10 more if possible.

Don't worry about considering if you have seen them recently or not.

At this point, your task is to generate as many names as you can.

When you have completed this task please go to the next step in this strategy.

Step Three: For illustrative purposes, we will use this drawing. It is basically a web with you at the center and four circles located on the web.

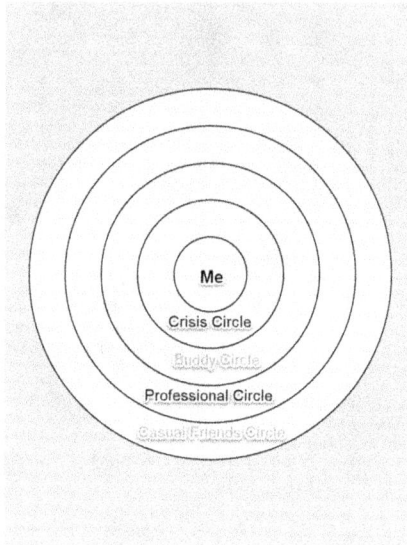

You should create a document with the names of the circles as your headings.

First Circle: The <u>Crisis Circle</u> is closest to the center of the Web.

These are the people you can really count on.

You should have at least four people who will be supportive in the event of death, illness, divorce or bankruptcy. They can include family, friends, your doctor or lawyer.

The Second Circle: This is your <u>buddy circle</u>.

Friends you have fun with, the people who accept you for who you are. There should be at least three people in this circle.

The Third Circle: This is your **professional circle**.

People who you know professionally, can provide reference letters and can speak about the quality of your work and character. You need at least 12 people in this category.

The Fourth Circle: This is your **casual friends** circle.

People you can share ideas with. You may work with them or know them through organizations or volunteer work. Some may become closer friends and eventually form part of the more inner and intimate circles.

NOW YOU HAVE SOME WORK TO DO.

Create a list of people under the four circle's headings e.g. My Crisis Circle... My Buddies Circle...

UP TO THIS POINT WE HAVEN'T FACTORED IN OUR LINKEDIN connections.

Likely, many of your Linkedin connections will fit into your Third Circle, your professional circle.

Once you have gone though your Linkedin connections, go through your other social media accounts and your e-mail address book and write down names.

You'll be surprised at how quickly the list grows.

We'll go into Linkedin in greater detail in an upcoming chapter in Part III.

In the next chapter, we learn how to leverage the connections you have just identified.

~

"PEOPLE BECOME REALLY QUITE REMARKABLE WHEN THEY START thinking that they can do things. When they believe in themselves they have the first secret of success." -- Norman Vincent Peale

"Use the Trial and Success method; learn how to improve and succeed by falling and learning from your mistakes." --- Brian Tracy

12. LEVERAGING YOUR CONNECTIONS

L everaging Your Connections:

IN THIS CHAPTER, WE DELVE DEEPER INTO NETWORKING AND HOW WE can leverage our connections as a powerful job searching strategy.

~

YOU MAY THINK YOU DON'T KNOW ANYONE WHO CAN HELP YOU WITH your job search. But you know more people than you think, and there's a very good chance at least a few of these people know someone who can give you career advice or point you to a job opening.

You'll never know if you don't ask!

Some Job Search Coaches will tell you leveraging your network is the most effective strategy you can use to find your ideal job.

The **Network Web** is a powerful tool. You'll be amazed at all the contacts you do have, and can identify the gaps in the network.

With your goal of finding suitable employment in mind you can ask:

- Who do I need to know?
- Who do I need to bring into my circle?
- And who do I know who can introduce them to me?

Reach out to your network.

All the connections in the world won't help you find a job if no one knows about your situation.

Once you've drawn up your list, start making contact with the people in your network. Let them know that you're looking for a job.

Be specific about what kind of work you're looking for and ask them if they have any information or know anyone in a relevant field.

Don't assume certain people won't be able to help. You may be surprised by who they know.

FIGURE OUT WHAT YOU <u>WANT</u> BEFORE YOU START NETWORKING.

Networking is most effective when you have specific employer targets and career goals. It's hard to get leads with a generic "Let me know if you hear of anything" request.

You may think you'll have better job luck if you leave yourself open to all the possibilities, but the reality is this 'openness' creates a black hole that sucks all the networking potential out of the connection.

A **generic** networking request for a job is worse than no request at all because you can lose a networking contact and opportunity.

Asking for **specific** information, leads, or an interview is much more focused and easier for the networking source.

If you're having trouble focusing your job search, you can turn to close friends and family members for help, but avoid contacting more distant people in your network until you've set clear goals.

START WITH YOUR REFERENCES.

When you are looking for a job, start with your references.

Your best references — the people who like you and can endorse your abilities, track record, and character--are major networking hubs. Contact each one of your references to network about your possibilities and affirm their agreement to be your reference.

HERE ARE A FEW QUICK POINTS FOR WORKING WITH YOUR REFERENCES:

- Describe your goals and seek their assistance.
- Keep them informed on your job search progress.
- Prepare them for any calls from potential employers.
- Let them know what happened and thank them for their help regardless of the outcome.

IF YOU'RE NERVOUS ABOUT MAKING CONTACT --- EITHER BECAUSE YOU'RE uncomfortable asking for favors or embarrassed about your employment situation--try to keep the following things in mind:

It feels good to help others. Most people will gladly assist you if they can. People like to give advice and be recognized for their expertise. Almost everyone knows what it's like to be out of work or looking for a job. They'll sympathize with your situation.

Unemployment can be isolating and stressful. By connecting with others, you're sure to get some much-needed encouragement, fellowship, and moral support. Reconnecting with the people in your network can be fun--even if you have an agenda.

The more this feels like a chore the more tedious and anxiety-ridden the process will be.

Focus on building relationships.

Networking is a give-and-take process that involves making connections, sharing information, and asking questions. It's a way of relating to others, not a technique for getting a job or a favour.

You don't need to hand out your business cards on street corners, cold call everyone on your contact list, or work a room of strangers. All you have to do is reach out.

Be authentic. In any job search or networking situation, being you-- the real you--should be your goal. Hiding who you are or suppressing your true interests and goals will only hurt you in the long run.

Pursuing what you want and not what you think others will like, will always be more fulfilling and ultimately more successful.

Be considerate. If you're reconnecting with an old friend or colleague, take the time to get through the catching-up phase before you blurt out your need. On the other hand, if this person is a busy professional you don't know well, be respectful of his or her time and come straight out with your request.

Ask for advice, not a job. Don't ask for a job, a request comes with a lot of pressure.

You want your contacts to become allies in your job search, not make them feel ambushed, so ask for information or insight instead. If they're able to hire you or refer you to someone who can, they will.

If not, you haven't put them in the uncomfortable position of turning you down or telling you they can't help. Be specific in your request.

BEFORE YOU GO OFF AND RECONNECT WITH EVERYONE YOU'VE EVER known, get your act together and do a little homework. Be prepared to articulate <u>what</u> you're looking for:

- Is it a reference?
- An insider's take on the industry?
- A referral?
- An introduction to someone in the field?

Also make sure to provide an update on your qualifications and recent professional experience.

SLOW DOWN AND ENJOY THE JOB NETWORKING PROCESS.

The best race car drivers are masters of slowing down.

They know the fastest way around the track is by slowing down going into the turns, so they can accelerate sooner as they're heading into the straightaway.

As you're networking, keep this "Slow in, fast out" racing mantra in mind. Effective networking is not something that should be rushed.

This doesn't mean you shouldn't try to be efficient and focused, but hurried, <u>emergency</u> networking is not conducive to building relationships for mutual support and benefit.

When you network, you should slow down, be present, and try to enjoy the process. This will speed up your chances for success in the job-hunting race.

Just because you have an agenda doesn't mean you can't enjoy reconnecting.

DON'T BE A HIT-AND-RUN NETWORKER

Don't be a hit-and-run networker: connecting, getting what you want, and then disappearing, never to be heard from until the next time you need something.

Invest in your network by following up and providing feedback to those who were kind enough to offer their help. Thank them for their referral and assistance. Let them know whether you got the interview or the job. Or use the opportunity to report on the lack of success or the need for additional help.

EVALUATE THE QUALITY OF YOUR NETWORK.

IF YOUR NETWORKING EFFORTS DON'T SEEM TO BE GOING ANYWHERE, YOU may need to evaluate the quality of your network. Take some time to think about your network's strengths, weaknesses and opportunities.

Without such an evaluation, there is little chance your network will adapt to your needs and your future goals. You may not notice how bound you are to history, or how certain connections are holding you back. And you may miss opportunities to branch out and forge new ties that will help you move forward.

Taking inventory of your network and where it is lacking is time well spent. If you feel your network is out of date, then it's time to upgrade! Your mere awareness of your needs will help you connect you with new and more relevant contacts and networks.

. . .

TAKE ADVANTAGE OF BOTH "STRONG" AND "WEAK" TIES

Everyone has both 'strong' and 'weak' ties.

Strong ties occupy your inner circle and weak ties are less established. Adding people to networks is time consuming, especially strong ties. It requires an investment of time and energy to have multiple 'best friends.' Trying to stay in touch with new acquaintances is just as challenging. But adding new 'weak tie' members gives your network vitality and even more cognitive flexibility--the ability to consider new ideas and options.

New relationships invigorate the network by providing a connection to new networks, viewpoints, and opportunities.

In the next chapter, we explore tips for strengthening your job search network.

∾

13. TIPS FOR STRENGTHENING YOUR JOB SEARCH NETWORK

T ips for Strengthening Your Job Search Network:

Tap into your strong ties. Your strong ties will logically and trustingly lead to new weak ties that build a stronger network.

Use your existing network to add members and reconnect with people. Start by engaging the people in your trusted inner circle to help you fill in the gaps in your network.

Think about where you want to go. Your network should reflect where you're going, not just where you've been. Adding people to your network who reflect issues, jobs, industries, and areas of interest is essential.

If you are a new graduate or a career changer, join the professional associations that represent your desired career path. Attending conferences, reading journals, and keeping up with the lingo of your desired field can prepare you for where you want to go.

Make the process of connecting a priority. Make connecting a habit--part of your lifestyle. Connecting is just as important as your exercise routine. It breathes life into you and gives you confidence.

Find out how your network is doing in this environment, what steps they are taking, and how you can help. As you connect, the world will feel smaller and a small world is much easier to manage.

TAKE THE TIME TO MAINTAIN YOUR NETWORK.

Maintaining your job-search network is just as important as building it.

Accumulating new contacts can be beneficial, but only if you have the time to nurture the relationships. Avoid the irrational impulse to meet as many new people as possible.

The key is quality rather than quantity. Focus on cultivating and maintaining your existing network. You're sure to discover an incredible array of information, knowledge, expertise, and opportunities.

SCHEDULE TIME WITH YOUR KEY CONTACTS.

LIST THE PEOPLE WHO ARE CRUCIAL TO YOUR NETWORK--PEOPLE YOU know who can and have been very important to you. Invariably, there will be some you have lost touch with.

Reconnect and then schedule a regular meeting or phone call. You don't need a reason to get in touch. It will always make you feel good and provide you with an insight or two.

. . .

PRIORITIZE THE REST OF YOUR CONTACTS.

Keep a running list of people you need to reconnect with. People whose view of the world you value. People you'd like to get to know better or whose company you enjoy.

Prioritize these contacts and then schedule time into your regular routine so you can make your way down the list.

TAKE NOTES ON THE PEOPLE IN YOUR NETWORK.

Collecting cards and filing them is a start. But maintaining your contacts, new and old, requires updates. Add notes about their families, their jobs, their interests, and their needs.

Unless you have a photographic memory, you won't remember all of this information unless you write it down. Put these updates and notes on the back of their business cards or input them into your contact database.

FIND WAYS TO RECIPROCATE

Always remember successful networking is a two-way street. Your ultimate goal is to cultivate mutually beneficial relationships.

That means giving as well as receiving.

Send a thank-you note, ask them about their family, email an article you think they might be interested in, and check in periodically to see how they're doing. By nurturing the relationship through your job search and beyond, you'll establish a strong network of people you can count on for ideas, advice, feedback, and support.

~

"IF YOU BELIEVE IN YOUR COMPANY, IF YOU BELIEVE IN YOUR PRODUCT, IF you believe in yourself; then you can march to success." -- Jeffrey Gitomer

"To succeed in sales, simply talk to lots of people every day. And here's what's exciting - there are lots of people!" --- Jim Rohn

14. HOW HIGH DOES YOUR ELEVATOR GO?

- 30 seconds? 60 seconds ... 10 minutes?
- Different buildings?

How High Does Your Elevator Go?

The buzzword for conducting business effectively in the new millennium may very well prove to be 'networking.' In turn, the key element of a networking interaction is the <u>elevator pitch</u> or <u>elevator speech</u> as some would call it. We used them as children... "you show me yours and I'll show you mine!"

Well perhaps not quite the same but at its essence it's an opportunity to show your stuff and to learn about the other person. Assuming they follow the rules of course.

The basic premise is to imagine you are sharing an elevator ride with a person who could be influential in advancing your business or career. You have the duration of the elevator ride to impress upon this individual why they should buy into your cause or at least agree to talk to you some more about it.

How long should my elevator pitch be? Good question! Answer... It depends. Not much of an answer at first glance, but it really depends on the norms or the culture for location or venue of the networking session. Presenting your 30 minute curriculum vitae wouldn't likely go over very well in a round-robin style of group introduction where the expectation is 30 seconds, not 30 minutes.

Many referral networking breakfast/luncheon groups based on the BNI (Business Networking International) model, limit their members to 30 second elevator pitches. The more members, the longer the activity takes, but at least it gives everyone an opportunity to speak.

A few years back I organized a series of Power Networking Breakfasts. It was speed networking at its best, very much like a speed dating concept. Participants were allowed two minutes and thirty seconds to deliver their pitch. Time limits were rigidly followed with Toastmasters style speech timing lights, green, amber and red and a bell to signal the speaker to stop their pitch, then on to the next pitcher. The pre-event promotional material advised the participant to come prepared with a two minute elevator pitch and to be prepared to answer a question or two about their pitch.

It was amazing to find that many of the participants faced challenges in trying to fill their two minutes. They had been programmed to stand up and speak and sit down within the restriction of 30 seconds.

I believe one of the challenges many of us face is we have been taught from an early age not to brag about ourselves. When it comes to business, if we don't promote ourselves or our business i.e. blow our own horn, then who will?

We should be passionate about our businesses and be able to talk at length about what we do, why we do it and why you should do business with us. In fact, I would challenge you to be prepared to deliver a 30-minute presentation about yourself and/or your business. Arguably that would likely be one of the slowest elevator rides ever, but if you have ever found yourself stuck in one for an extended period of time, you will know that it could very well happen.

A challenge I face is with having multiple business ventures, volunteer roles, my professional career & pursuits, I could easily take the full thirty minutes for my 30-second pitch allotment. That doesn't leave any room for the others. If you find yourself in a similar situation I think that the answer lays in referring back to our analogy of the elevator ride.

Many larger high rises have more than one elevator. I would challenge you to create multiple elevator pitches you can use to match with the appropriate venue and situation. A social setting may be a good place to talk about some of the activities you are involved with and touching upon, but not going heavily into what you do for a living.

At a Toastmasters conference I would likely introduce myself as...

"Good morning everyone, I'm Rae Stonehouse. I'm a Distinguished Toastmaster and have been a member for over twenty-five years. So far! I've served as our District 21 Governor a few years back and continue to serve our leaders in multiple roles. My passion is organizing and creating something from nothing. I'd love to hear how your Toastmasters experience has been. Rae Stonehouse."

I've kept it short and sweet and hopefully have piqued someone's interest that they would want to talk to me some more. I haven't mentioned my profession or my business ventures at all. I will likely fit that into the follow-up conversation as the opportunity arises.

Here's an example of an elevator pitch that wouldn't be such a good idea. Let's say I was in a meeting of the senior managers in my organization. It would probably not be well received if I were to give an introductory pitch highlighting my experience as a union activist. It would be much better to identify my name, my professional designation, where I work, how long and what I bring to the table.

I'm a firm believer in the adage "If the only tool you have in your toolbox is a hammer, then every problem will be a nail." I believe that to be an effective networker you need to have a selection of tools in your metaphorical toolbox. Having a selection of elevator pitches to be able to rely on for any situation is one such tool. Don't throw away that hammer though. Sometimes a hammer is exactly what is needed!

～

15. DEVELOPING YOUR ELEVATOR
     PITCH

Y ou need to develop your elevator pitch like you would a formal presentation. Just because you are introducing yourself conversationally in a 1 to 1 or a small group doesn't mean that you should wing it.

Preparation is the key to your success. Remember you should be prepared for different lengths of elevator rides and different situations.

Follow these steps to develop your unique pitch.

DESCRIBE YOURSELF AS A SOLUTION TO A PROBLEM:

The most important part of your elevator pitch is your opening sentence. You need to grab your audience's attention by telling what is unique about what you do.

In your very first sentence you need to say your name, your business' name and describe yourself as a solution to the problems your clients, customers or business associates face. Listeners don't usually care about your job title as much as what you can do for them.

When creating the first line of your elevator pitch, put yourself in the audience's shoes and answer the age old question "What's in it for me?"

A superior elevator pitch increases your heart rate. It speaks to who you really are and what excites you about your business. If you don't get excited about it, who will?

Your pitch needs to address the five Ws:

The first step is to develop answers to the following questions:

1. What does your business do? (For example, begin your answer with "We provide...")
2. Whom does your business do it for? (For example, begin your answer with "For small and mid-sized healthcare providers.")
3. Why do they care? Or, What's in it for them? (For example, include in your answer "so that they can...," "who can no longer afford...," or "who are tired of...")
4. Why is your business different? (For example, begin your answer with "As opposed to..." or "Unlike...")
5. What is your business? (For example, begin your answer with "My business is an insurance against...")

Don't forget to include your **USP**, your hook. It is a good way to close off your elevator pitch. For example, using my business... Mr. Emcee Your Okanagan Event Planner of Choice. From start to finish... we do it all!

Tell an anecdote: (for longer pitches):

After you describe the problems you solve, tell a short story to explain your motivation for doing what you do. This story should be something exciting... the aha! moment where you realized that you had to do what you do. Or you could tell a story that illustrates how exceptionally good you are at your craft.

Start a dialogue:

Conclude your pitch with an open-ended question... one that can't be answered with a simple "yes" or "no" answer. Closing with a question can draw the listener in, serving as a foundation for a deeper conversation and collaboration, and eventually, a relationship.

Make sure you prepare, rehearse and regularly revise your elevator pitch to effectively market yourself and capitalize on opportunities that come your way --- whether you are in an elevator or not!

Here are some important considerations to keep in mind.

- Don't confuse people with your pitch. No one needs to hear your entire work history on first meeting you.
- No matter how tough it's been you don't need to tell a sob story, paint a positive picture. You need to be congruent with your professional image. As they say you need to **walk your talk**. If you are marketing yourself as a wellness coach it would not work for you if you were sick quite often or were carrying 20 to 30 extra pounds.

~

16. ELEVATOR PITCH TEMPLATE

O pening Salutation: (Good morning, good afternoon, good evening)

Your Name:

Your Business Name:

USP: (what is unique about what you do?)

(How are you a solution to the problem?

Closing Comments: (Repeat your name & business name and add a hook)

** For longer time allowances factor in an anecdote and/or close by starting a dialogue.

An example of a short elevator pitch I have used is as follows:

"Hello everyone. I am Rae Stonehouse aka Mr. Emcee and I am a cat juggler! Metaphorically of course! As an event organizer and promoter I have multiple cats in the air at the same time. Sometimes they go the way they are supposed to, most of the time they don't. My job is to make those cats fly in formation. I provide organization for the many details that accompany an event and provide my clients peace of mind. Unless they have an allergy to cats of course. Rae Stonehouse... Mr. Emcee... your Okanagan Valley event organizer & promoter of choice. From start to finish... we do it all!"

Power Networking Logistics

1. Develop your elevator pitch first sentence i.e. who you & your business are.
2. Answer the question "What does your business do?"
3. Add your USP?
4. Create an anecdote to explain why you do what you do.
5. Develop a list of open-ended questions that you could use to keep the conversation going.
6. Develop a 30-second elevator pitch.
7. Develop a 60-second elevator pitch.

17. IT'S ALL ABOUT YOU!

- Questions that you **will** answer
- Questions that you **won't** answer
- Your Questions Toolbox

Q UESTIONS YOU SHOULD ANSWER

You should be prepared to answer questions about your business or yourself that are legitimate fact-finding questions. After all, who knows more about you or your business than you do? Some questions that come to mind:

- How long have you been in business?
- Do you work alone or do you have others with you?
- Where did you get the idea for your business?
- Had you worked in the industry before you started your business?
- Has it been successful for you?
- Have you experienced any successes or setbacks that you would like to share with us?

I think you get the idea. I would suggest you brainstorm your own list of possible questions somebody could ask you and then create an answer for each of those questions.

I find one example of a situation that creates anxiety in shy people is when they are caught by surprise with a question they are not prepared or are expecting to answer. If it is your business, you really shouldn't be caught by surprise!

A good example to illustrate this point was the late Robin Williams, the comedian. He always seemed to have a rapid-fire response for any question presented to him or a situation that arose. It would appear he was quick witted in his response and making them up on the spot but in reality he was extremely well prepared. His impromptu i.e. on the spur of the moment comments were well rehearsed. He had one prepared for almost every situation where he can recall and recite it very quickly. You should do the same when asked questions about yourself or your business. Don't be caught off guard!

QUESTIONS YOU SHOULDN'T ANSWER

THERE ARE RUDE PEOPLE OUT THERE WHO WILL ASK QUESTIONS THAT are none of their business, yet they will ask anyways. You need to be prepared with an answer that informs them politely it really isn't any of their business. There are also people who are merely inquisitive and don't realize they are asking a question they shouldn't be.

Once again I would suggest brainstorming a list of questions you would not want to answer and prepare for them.

A few come to mind:

- How much income did you make last year?
- How much income tax did you pay last year?
- Why did you fire... ?

There is a style of question you need to be aware of in case you encounter it and that is the "no win" question. Its intent is to do you harm in some way. An example would be "Is it true that you have stopped beating your wife?"

To answer "Yes" would imply that you do beat your wife. To answer "No" would be equally as incriminating as it would indicate that you are still beating her.

A suggested technique to deflect an awkward or embarrassing question is to reply "I wonder why you would ask a question like that?" It takes the power away from the questioner and causes them to justify their own inappropriate question.

~

YOUR QUESTIONS TOOLBOX

I believe I mentioned earlier the value of having different tools available for you to use at different times. Effective communication skills are an asset.

One of the challenges many shy people have occurs in the small talk phase of an interpersonal interaction. The same can apply in a networking scenario where your colleague has delivered their elevator pitch and you yours. What comes next?

If your conversational partner is a skilled communicator you can go along for the ride, if not, it will likely be up to you to take the lead. "But I'm shy" you say. "I can't do that!" Shyness is about not having the skills you need in a social situation and it often leads to fear. If you are prepared in advance and have practiced the skills, you reduce the likelihood you will trigger your anxiety. The intent here is you develop a list of questions that allow you to progress the discussion, learn more about the other individual without seeming you are grilling them with your questions.

Here are some examples of questions that can help progress a conversation. I urge you to develop your own, especially ones that feel comfortable for you to use.

- Tell me about your business?
- How is your year/month/week going so far?
- How did you ever get into this business?
- Did you have any experience in this line of work before you actually opened up your own business?
- Have you ever been to one of these networking events before?
- Do you have any advice you would share with me about business?
- What are you most proud of with your business?
- How do you see the future of your field or industry?
- How do you foresee the future for your business?

Of course, any of these questions may be on the other's list of questions they have chosen not to answer. You won't know until you ask them and who knows where the conversation takes itself as you learn more. You will need to learn to ask more questions based on the answers you receive and how to interject your own experience on the matter into the discussion. This gets easier with practice.

∾

18. TECHNOLOGY REVISITED

- Your e-mail signature file
- Your personal domain name
- Your voice mail message

YOUR E-MAIL SIGNATURE

A relatively easy way of promoting yourself is to develop an e-mail signature file that not only provides your contact information, it also allows you to promote yourself. E-mail signatures can easily be set up using Outlook, assuming you are using Outlook and a word processing program.

I've provided examples of some of the ones I use below. I believe you should have a signature file for every 'persona' you have. One of the techniques I use to self-promote is that after I have been communicating with an individual on a particular subject and under a specific signature file, I will accidentally i.e. on purpose, send my message with a different signature file. This is a sneaky way of letting someone know I have other interests or services to supply. Whether it works or not, I really don't know.

Your signature file is like a small billboard that promotes you. You should make it as easy as possible for people to contact you. If you have a website, provide the url so the reader of your e-mail can easily navigate to it. Make sure it has been hyperlinked i.e. when they click on the link it will take them to the website.

I am not currently using it on any of my signature files but many people insert a link to their Linkedin profile if they feel that there is value in doing so.

Don't forget to add a head-shot photo of yourself. I expand on the subject elsewhere in this book. I often get the comment "Oh, I recognize you from your e-mail." For a shy networker this can be quite helpful. In theory, people will walk up to you and say "I know you!"

Rae Stonehouse aka Mr. Emcee
250-451-6564
rae@mremcee.com
mremcee.com
Your Okanagan Event Organizer & Master of Ceremonies of Choice
Check out our blog E=EmceeSquared
From start to finish ... we do it all!

MR. EMCEE

Rae Stonehouse,
Chairman of the Board
Okanagan Valley Entrepreneurs Society (OVES)
PO Box 140-1876 Cooper Rd. Unit 138
Kelowna, B.C., V1Y 9N6
250-451-6564

rae@okanaganentrepreneurs.ca
okanaganentrepreneurs.ca

"OVES... Driving the Entrepreneurial Spirit"

District 21 Toastmasters
Where Leaders Are Made

Rae Stonehouse DTM PDG
D21 Toastmasters Webmaster
rae.stonehouse@d21toastmasters.org
d21toastmasters.org
250-451-6564

"Attitude Still Equals Altitude!"

Rae Stonehouse
Okanagan Help 4 Biz
250-451-6564
rae@okanaganhelp4biz.ca
okanaganhelp4biz.ca

Okanagan Help 4 Biz

"Your Business Solutions Resource"

Rae A. Stonehouse DTM
Author, Writer, Speaker & Self-Publishing Coach/Consultant
Live For Excellence Productions (LFEP)

Contact: 250-451-6564 publishme@liveforexcellence.com
Visit liveforexcellence.com for more info.

Live For Excellence Productions

To learn more about Rae, visit the Wonderful World of Rae Stonehouse.

So how do we create a signature file within Outlook?

From within Outlook click on **File**. (This demonstration is using Outlook 2010.)

Next click on **Options**. Then **Mail**.

Locate and click on **Signatures**.

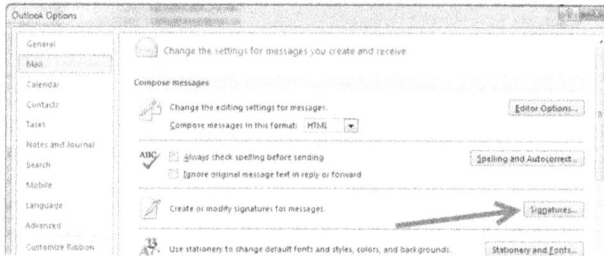

YOU WILL THEN OPEN THE **SIGNATURES AND STATIONERY** BOX. IF THIS IS your first time, there won't be any info displayed.

Locate and click on the **New** button. You will be prompted to **Type a name for this signature**. Use something that makes sense to you if you will be developing multiple signatures.

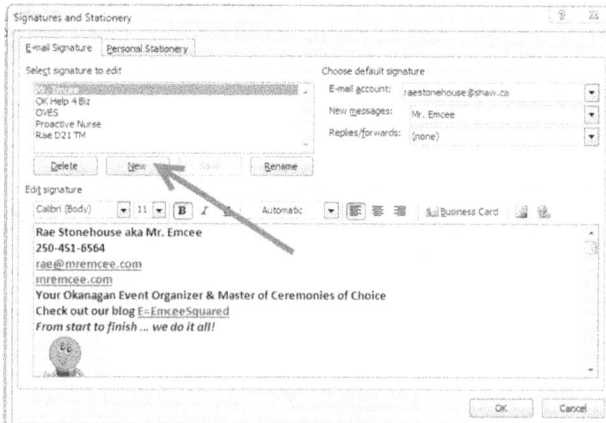

The **Edit signature** box allows you to insert your contact & promotional information. The arrow on the left in illustration above allows you to insert a photo of yourself. When you click on it, it will prompt you to add a graphic from your computer to your signature file. This step can be tedious as you might have to add your photo, save it, then open up a new message in Outlook to see if your photo is in the right scale i.e. not too small, not too large.

The second arrow allows you to add a hyperlink to any text in your message. You would highlight the text you want to be hyperlinked and click on the globe icon. You will then be prompted for the next steps.

When you have your info the way that you want it, click on **OK**, which is the same as saving. The next step would be to open up a new message in your Outlook to see how it looks.

I mentioned above that you need to ensure your photo is to scale i.e. in relation to the rest of your signature. Another consideration is how the photo is situated related to the text. Outlook does not do a good job of placing a photo with the accompanying text. It doesn't look like what you see in the **Edit Signature** box. The workaround is to locate the signature files that Outlook saved on your hard drive and open them in Word. You can do this by using the Search function in Microsoft Explorer, which searches your directories for files with the name that you have provided. Once you locate the file, open it in Word and you can use the photo positioning features in Word to wrap the text around your photo. I always have my photo justified to the left with the text blocked to the right i.e. the text starts at the top of the graphic and works towards the bottom.

~

YOUR PERSONAL DOMAIN

If you are able to create and develop websites, you should obtain a domain in your name e.g. raestonehouse.com. This is a good place to upload promotional material about yourself. Even if you don't have website development skills it is worth your while to obtain a domain in your name for a couple reasons:

1) so nobody else does and

2) just in case you want to develop a website in your name at a later date. If you have a name that is relatively common you may find this step difficult as somebody else may have taken it.

~

YOUR VOICE MAIL MESSAGE

In this chapter I have been suggesting using technology to promote yourself. Two different concepts come to mind here. One, being drawn from the field of marketing. You apparently need to touch your customer 7 to 11 times before they will do business with you. Now that doesn't mean that you physically touch them. Doing so may very well may cause you some problems you weren't expecting.

A touch or more precisely a 'touch point' is every time your potential customer is exposed to your name and business. An advertisement in the newspaper they have seen would be considered as one touch point, assuming they saw and read the ad. A second might be they have heard a radio ad you have running. This is how brand recognition works. They need to hear your name over and over again to recognize it. Having a voice mail message that promotes your business when somebody phones it would be considered a touch point.

Secondly, and we will talk about this elsewhere in this book is people do make snap decisions on you upon first contact. A poorly created and spoken voice mail message will do you more harm than benefit.

Your message should be courteous and welcoming as well as providing information as to when you will get back to the individual or perhaps alternative contact methods. You could also add your tagline or USP to your message. Have some fun with it!

Power Networking Logistics

1. Develop a list of questions you <u>will</u> answer.
2. Create answers for these questions.
3. Develop a list of questions you <u>won't</u> answer.
4. Prepare a response for questions you <u>won't</u> answer.
5. Prepare a list of open-ended questions you can use to advance a conversation.
6. Create an e-mail signature file for each of your personas.
7. Purchase a domain name for your name.
8. If you have website development skills, create a website in your name.
9. Customize your voice mail message.

19. LIVE FACE-TO-FACE NETWORKING PHASE

- Types of Pitching Opportunities
- Your Elevator has Arrived: What do you talk about?
- Coffee anyone?
- Who's Next?
- Dress for success
- Business Card Presentation & Etiquette
- Wear a Name Tag
- Whole lotta shaking going on
- Maintaining Eye Contact
- Obstacles to Communicating/Networking: Close Encounters of the Shy Kind

TYPES OF PITCHING OPPORTUNITIES

WE HAVE TALKED PREVIOUSLY ABOUT DEVELOPING DIFFERENT LENGTHS of elevator pitches and different types to promote whatever aspect of you or your business you want to highlight. In upcoming chapters we will discuss having a one-to-one conversation after you deliver your elevator pitch.

In this chapter I want to focus on different situations/opportunities you may encounter that will call upon you to deliver your pitch.

My local Chamber of Commerce has initiated what they call a <u>power networking</u> opportunity and liken it to speed dating. The format is that a certain amount of the early bird attendees at their Business After Hours form a large circle. Somebody from the Chamber Administration serves as the facilitator and goes around the room having everybody deliver a 30-second pitch. I've participated in a few of them and have noticed the same people being ineffective in their delivery or squirming because they are uncomfortable. I have also seen some who seem to think that 30 seconds is the same as ten minutes and go on and on. Either they don't clue in or they think rules are for other people, I say as I stand on my soapbox.

My approach to this scenario is to deliver my 30-second elevator pitch and try to stand out from the others, hoping to them to come up and talk to me after the activity is over. One technique I use is I always start off with a salutation. Example: "Good morning everyone" or "good evening everyone", depending on the time of day of course. I believe that it demonstrates I am confident in what I am saying next.

Another tip I have learned is in how I announce my name. Many people are focused on what they are going to say themselves and find it difficult to remember the other person's name, let alone their own. Try saying your first name, followed by a pause then your first and second name. Example: "Good morning everyone. I'm Rae... Rae Stonehouse..." Try it a few times to see how it feels.

This is a variation on how 007 introduces himself... "Bond... James Bond." Don't forget to use your name though and not his or mine.

Here's another common scenario I have seen used as an icebreaker activity to start off a small group activity. You are asked to interview the person beside you and introduce them to the group. In essence, you are delivering their elevator pitch for them. The challenge is there never seems to be enough time for the exercise and not only do you have to collect their information, you also have to make sure you have delivered your pitch to your partner and verify they actually heard you.

I would recommend using pen and paper to jot down some notes about your partner. This will help you keep track of the details you want to share. I try to keep my notes simple by capturing their name (it is surprising to see how many people actually stumble over this part), the name of their business and an interesting point or two about the individual.

When delivering my introduction of my partner I always use the same format.

"Good morning/evening everyone. It gives me great pleasure to introduce the lady/gentleman seated to my right/left. They operate a business called.... and they provide.... Please welcome....!

I often receive favorable comments on these introductions and it demonstrates my confidence and poise. However, when my partner introduces me, I really don't have any control of how they deliver my introduction and hope they don't butcher it. I believe the introduction I give can help mitigate any damage my partner does in their introduction of me.

～

20. YOUR ELEVATOR HAS ARRIVED: WHAT DO YOU TALK ABOUT?

I t's showtime! Meeting somebody for the first time as in a networking situation can often leave you stuck for words. Your counterpart delivers their elevator pitch and then as they pause to catch their breath they utter "so what do you do?" You go on to deliver your well-rehearsed pitch for your business. But did the two of you really communicate?

Communication is a two way process. While the other person is sharing their story, you need to be listening closely to them. This isn't the time to be practicing your own story in your head. This is the time to listen. Imagine there will be a test after your partner delivers their personal story. Besides trying to figure out what their business is about, you should be listening for statements or beliefs similar to yours. Perhaps you have had similar experiences as they have described.

Research has shown people like to do business with people who are similar to themselves. It is also often said people will do business with friends before strangers. So how do you rapidly turn an impromptu exchange of elevator pitches into a 'best buddies' scenario?

Well, sometimes it does happen by accident. You meet somebody and very rapidly find you 'hit it off' as the saying goes. If you are a Law of Attraction follower, you would say you are resonating. You are on the same wave length. But more often than naught it doesn't go that way and can be awkward at best.

The solution lays in you taking charge of the conversation. By charge, I don't mean to take control and dominate it at the other's expense. I mean to be proactive and direct the conversation in the way you want it to go. Research has shown most people respond well when you ask them questions about something they have just said, asking them to expand upon a point perhaps. The usual questions of <u>who</u>, <u>how</u>, <u>why</u>, <u>when</u> and <u>where</u> can be used to elicit further info effectively as long as you don't come across as giving them the third degree. "Where were you on the night of...? Can anybody vouch for your where-abouts?" may not be the way to win friends and influence people.

Asking more questions of the person is also a highly recommended traditional sales communication method i.e. you use the information you have just gathered to tailor your sales pitch for the individual. While it may be okay if you are actually in a sales situation I wouldn't recommend it in first-contact networking encounter. As I said <u>most</u> people will respond well to probing questions as long as they feel you are eager to learn more from them. You will know fairly quickly if you are dealing with a paranoid individual. They are out there.

Once you determine whether you have common interests, don't forget to talk about the possibility of doing business together or helping each other with referrals.

Who knows, you may start off business networking and end up with a new best friend.

~

21. COFFEE ANYONE?

We have been talking about talking. You can only fit so much into a conversation at a networking event and you really shouldn't try to overdo it. Get agreement in principal to meet for coffee. If your conversational partner doesn't make the offer, you should. This is assuming of course that you see the value in meeting this individual for further exploration of common interests. You may not see any value and they the same. Coffee chat isn't mandatory.

EVEN THOUGH MANY PEOPLE CARRY SMART PHONES NOWADAYS, THEY ARE likely not eager to check their schedule, at that very moment, to see when they can meet.

IF YOU HAVE RECEIVED A BUSINESS CARD FROM THEM IT WOULD BE OKAY to write a short note on the back of it to remind you to contact them and possibly the best time to do so if you are phoning them.

IN THE NEXT SECTION, THE POST NETWORKING PHASE, WE EXPLORE how and why you should follow-up with your contacts.

22. WHO'S NEXT?

You have had a good chat with someone and you feel there is a chance of possibilities developing. You part and go your separate ways. Now what?

Some books on networking I have read would say you should plan your 'attack' in advance. Attack would seem to be a little strong of a word. Approach might be better.

If you recognize friends at the networking event, should you stop to speak to them? While one answer might be "No, you already know them, you should be networking with people that you don't know. "Another, more effective answer, would be, "Yes, certainly!"

"Networking is a lot like gardening." I'm not sure if anybody famous has said that so I will take credit for it. Relationships need to be nurtured. We all have business colleagues or business friends that while we don't necessarily do business with them, we see them regularly at business networking sessions. 'Catching up' is a good way to learn more about the business environment from a different perspective than your own.

It's also a great way to put the word out on what you require for your business or what you have to offer someone else to advance theirs.

People will do business with those they know and care about before they will with someone they don't. Like watering your garden, business relationships need to be nurtured.

I wouldn't suggest spending too much time with them though as doing so would prevent either of you from the networking for new contacts that you likely attended the event for. This would be another opportunity to set a coffee date if you are wanting to chat at greater length or depth.

Leveraging your colleague's connections can be an effective networking technique. By asking "Is there anyone here that you know and could introduce me to that could help me with...?" And if there is, have them seek out the referral and make the introduction.

If you are shy and reluctant to meet people for the first time, having a colleague or friend walk with you to make the first contact can take a lot of pressure off you.

~

23. DRESS FOR SUCCESS:

M ost of us have likely been told from a very early age "You shouldn't judge a book by its cover." Yet we do it every day, often in the first few seconds of having met someone. We automatically determine whether they are a danger to us, whether we would want to have a conversation with them, whether we would want them as a mate... or to mate with. We do it automatically.

It's part of being human and our judgement is often made with the clothing the person is wearing as one of our decision making criteria. Being dressed wrong for a given situation can set you apart so that people do not want to approach you to converse. Remember, as a shy person, having somebody come up to you to talk can be a lot easier than having to make the approach yourself. So don't reduce your chances by dressing wrong.

Dressing wrong? What does that mean? There is a lot of room for interpretation. What is wrong for one person is right for another. Many people like to express themselves through colourful clothing or cutting edge fashion. Many people don't have a clue when it comes to dressing for the occasion. I attended a black tie gala awards event. I was wearing a tuxedo as was my colleague. We observed some men in their cleanest blue jeans with a black string tie. I think they missed the point.

My suggestion would be if you were attending a business networking event, then 'business casual' would be appropriate. This can become even more casual in hot climates. If everyone is wearing shorts and you are in your tuxedo, you may get attention but perhaps not the kind that you wanted.

As for dressing for success, it has been proven over and over that most people feel better about themselves when they are dressed up. You need every advantage that you can get when you are out there networking, marketing yourself. Don't shut the door in your face before it is even opened. People do judge others by their clothing, don't let them judge you without talking to you first.

～

24. BUSINESS CARD PRESENTATION & ETIQUETTE

I f you are planning on some serious networking you should have business cards available to present. Not having a card may be a missed opportunity for you. Besides serving as an introduction for you and your business they will serve as a visual prompt to remind the other person they met and spoke to you.

Business cards are quite inexpensive to print nowadays, so cost shouldn't be a deterrent to having some printed. If you are in transition and expect your info to change soon, your printer will likely accommodate small batch runs.

Even if you are technically not in business, perhaps in transition and looking for employment, you should still have a card that outlines who you are and what you do or the kind of work that you are looking for and how someone can get in contact with you.

Some business people believe in having their photo as part of the card. Supposedly, I'm guessing here, so you remember them better. It can be problematic if they have used a more youthful picture from yesteryear. We joke about some of the realtor's (real estate agents) business cards and newspaper advertisements we see locally. Their public marketing image is a young youthful person and when you meet them they are somewhat prune looking i.e. dried up and aged! I feel I have been tricked. Vanity can affect people in different ways I suppose.

The Japanese take the presentation of a business card in a one-to-one networking situation far more serious than we do. To them, ritual is involved. When presented with a business card you are expected to accept it with both hands, hold it in front of you and read the content of the card, both sides. You would then hold it with respect as the other person shares their elevator pitch. You would only place it in your pocket after you had left the person and you would never deface the card by writing on it.

In North America we are a little less respectful. Sometimes, quite a bit! I have met a fellow who within the first seconds of meeting him he announces "Well let's get this out of the way" and hands me his card. I expect that he wasn't as comfortable or skilled at networking as he thought that he was.

I have also seen an influential woman walk up to a group of people and start passing out her business cards. "Here you go, one for you and one for you!" She then left the group and went over to another and repeated the process. It was like she was feeding chickens or passing out candy to children who were trick or treating at her door. The purpose of passing out her business card seemed to be missed. I wonder if she was actually shy and was covering up her uncomfortableness?

So what is the correct way to present your card to another? How and when?

I'm sure everybody has their own view on the matter.

When I have been offered another's business card as part of an introduction that is under way, I will adopt what I described earlier as the Japanese method. I will accept it, quickly read the details and I will keep it in my hand in full view. I see the offering of a business card from another as the cue to offer mine in return. I often make a comment about a detail or an aspect of their business card to reinforce that I have taken a serious look at it.

If I don't see any action from my partner towards offering their business card I will initiate it myself. Asking, "Do you have a business card?" can be easier than saying "Here is my business card." Of course, their providing a card opens it up for me to provide mine.

I will also listen for a verbal cue of "I should get in contact with you", "I will keep in touch" or anything close to that as a signal for me to offer my card.

In an earlier section I mentioned the value of having different elevator pitches available for a given situation. At a business networking event I am prepared to give business cards as the discussion develops. After getting my own cards mixed up far too many times with the cards that I have received I have developed my own system of organization.

I usually wear a blazer with hip pockets. In my left pocket I would have a supply of my business cards. In my right pocket I have, a card representing my role as the Chairman of the Board of our local entrepreneurs society. In my wallet, I will carry some cards that I can pass out related to Toastmasters.

When I receive a new business card, after reading it I will insert it into my shirt pocket. As I have several blazers or suit coats I organize them all the same way. We will talk about name badges elsewhere, but I carry one in each blazer so that it will be there when I need it.

If I am expecting to pass out more than the average amount of business cards at an event I will have an extra supply in my briefcase or my vehicle should I require them.

A female reader of the last paragraph pointed out to me "What if you are wearing a little black dress and carrying a clutch purse, where do you put the cards that you have collected?" Having never worn a "little black dress" I can only assume that they don't include deep pockets.

Perhaps wearing the dress in the first place to a business networking event might be the point to focus on. I make no proclamation of being an expert on women's fashion!

I will even muddy the water a little and ask "Should you give your business card in all situations?"

I've been in interactions where the other individual doesn't seem overly interested in me, or are overly interested in themselves. I may make a judgement call on the spot and choose not to share my business card.

Then there are those who choose not to share business cards. This could be a simple matter of not having their cards printed yet or having problems deciding what to put on the card. Not everybody is creative.

I've heard of one woman who when asked for her business card replies "Oh, I don't do business cards. I prefer to write down the person's name and contact information on my little pad. It's much more personal."

It may be more personal to her, but in today's fast-paced world, this could be an irritant or an imposition to some networkers.

I'm reminded of a young fellow who attended one of my speed networking events I mentioned earlier. He was a salesman for a high-end office furniture business. When I asked him why he didn't have any business cards he replied "How could anybody forget this smiling face?"

Well, apparently they did. The next time I saw him he was behind the counter of our local Dairy Queen filling ice cream cones.

25. WEAR A NAME TAG

M any networking events you attend will provide a sticky-backed name tag with something like "Hello, my name is..." If the organizers are insistent that you wear it, I would suggest you write your name as interestingly as you can, something that will attract another to focus on it.

MY PREFERENCE WOULD BE TO WEAR A NAME BADGE THAT professionally displays my name and my business/organization. I believe people tend to scan your name badge when they are first approaching you to see if there is an immediate connection between you and them.

THEY CAN ALSO LOOK AT IT WHILE THEY ARE SPEAKING TO YOU TO KEEP your name in their mind. It can also help as a reminder to yourself if you get to the point where you are so overwhelmed with other's names and the networking process that you can look down and remind yourself what yours is.

· · ·

HERE ARE A COUPLE BADGES I HAD MADE FOR MY WIFE AND ME FOR MY business. I purchased two for myself so I could keep one in each of my sports jacket. I was surprised at how inexpensive they were to purchase i.e. $45.00 for three badges.

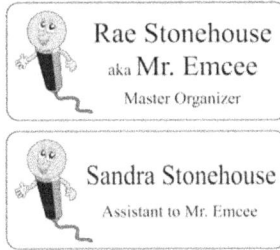

IN THIS CASE, THE TERM MASTER ORGANIZER, SETS SOMEBODY UP FOR the inevitable question of "So what do you organize?"

26. WHOLE LOTTA SHAKING GOING ON

A handshake is more than just a greeting. It is also a message about your personality and confidence level. In business, a handshake is an important tool in making the right first impression.

Before extending your hand, introduce yourself. Extending your hand should be part of an introduction, not a replacement for using your voice. This isn't the cue to start reciting your elevator pitch though. Extending your hand without saying anything may make you appear nervous or overly aggressive.

On one hand (pun intended!) it would seem that shaking someone's hand should be an easy process. We have likely been doing it most of our adult life. On the other hand, some people seem to have problems with it.

I believe part of the problem that creates anxiety is we over think things sometimes. We are anxious because we give more importance to the activity than it really deserves and it takes on a life of its own... creating anxiety. A self-fulfilling prophesy if there ever was one.

Another part that likely creates anxiety is we can only control our portion of the interaction. If our partner is an experienced handshaker, then all should go smoothly but many aren't.

There are a few different hand-shaking styles that come up in the literature and I am sure you have likely experienced them yourselves.

I personally don't like grasping someone's hand who has the so-called 'wet fish' handshake. It can leave you with an obsessive urge to wipe your hand as soon as you can, but fight the urge.

Even worse, there are times that my hand is sweating and I don't want the label. I have developed the habit of giving my hand a quick, unobtrusive wipe on my pant leg before offering my hand.

Then there is 'bone-crusher Bill.' The offered hand often comes in as curve from the hip of Bill with the express purpose of crushing walnuts. Or so it would seem. Bill never seems to realize the pain that he causes in others or the fact that people start to avoid him. Word can get around!

Another ineffective handshake I call the 'royal' handshake. Someone only offers you the tips of their fingers and no matter how hard you try you can't seem to grasp more than a few fingers. You are left feeling that you were robbed.

The bottom line is to avoid being any of these profiles. If you need to practice at home before going to a networking session, do so.

It seems to becoming more common that friends are hugging when meeting in a social setting. There are many people I call "huggy" people. I would suggest waiting to see if you are offered one rather than expecting one. It could make for an awkward situation if you were to offer a hug on a first contact and have it rejected.

∾

27. MAINTAINING EYE CONTACT

M any people have challenges maintaining eye contact with their conversational partner at the best of times. This can have different reasons. For some cultures it is inappropriate to look another in the eyes. Avoiding eye contact can be a sign of respect or deference to the other.

For the most part, maintaining eye contact in a conversation can demonstrate confidence. A couple challenges come to mind though. A difference in height between the speakers can be challenging, probably more for the short person looking up than the taller person looking down.

Another challenge in a busy room is to focus on your conversational partner, not on people passing by or other conversations going on. It can distract you and give the impression you are looking for a better conversation to join. If your partner is displaying this particular behaviour they too may well be scanning the room for a better opportunity.

While inadequate eye contact can work against you in a 1 to 1 conversation, what about too much eye contact?

I believe many of us have been on the receiving end of an intense stare. One where your conversational partner stares directly into your eyes and won't release you. It can feel painful. You may feel you are being put under a spell and are unable to look away. It may be an act of trying to control you, or it may be your conversational partner doesn't possess the social skill of maintaining eye contact in social conversation.

My career has been in psychiatry/mental health. An intense, out of the ordinary stare, may indicate mental health issues to me.

~

28. OBSTACLES TO COMMUNICATING/NETWORKING: CLOSE ENCOUNTERS OF THE SHY KIND

As this is a book on developing networking skills for shy people, I'm assuming you experience shyness to a certain degree. There isn't a standard measurement that applies to everyone. We all experience it in a different way. What might intimidate me may not cause any distress to you at all.

For some people it is the large groups of people that cause their anxiety. For others, it can be the inevitable 1 to 1 conversation, where they fear they may appear to be stupid.

For me, I find approaching somebody I don't know to be challenging. I would suspect I have a deep-seated fear of rejection triggering my anxiety. Yet, I have developed an advanced skill at public speaking, an area many would find to be even more stressful.

Darren Lacroix, a former Toastmasters International World Champion of Public Speaking Winner says one of the secrets to becoming an effective public speaker is "stage time, stage time, stage time." Translation: you just have to do it over and over again to become better.

I believe the same principal applies to becoming a better networker. The more you network, the more likely you will become more comfortable with doing so. There is an expression that says "practice makes perfect." It isn't true! If you keep making the same mistakes over and over again, you just become better at making mistakes.

Conversely, practice with constructive feedback can lead towards perfection. The Toastmasters International Program is based upon that very principal. I have been a member for over 25 years at the time of writing and I have experienced first-hand the benefits of constructive feedback.

When you are networking there isn't somebody watching you so you will have to evaluate yourself as to how you did. This can be challenging as we tend to be self-critical especially in areas where we experience anxiety.

~

29. NETWORKING SKILLS SELF-ASSESSMENT

I would suggest developing your own benchmark performance standards so you can compare each new meeting or interaction. You would conduct this exercise later on after the event was finished. Questions lead to yes or no answers. Others may be better answered on a sliding scale. If you keep records of your results you are better able to track your progress.

Some examples might be:

- I approached someone I didn't know and made the first comment. Yes - No
- I listened intently while the other person delivered their elevator pitch before starting mine.
- I was able to deliver my elevator speech comfortably.
- I was able to maintain eye contact for much of our discussion.
- I initiated an invitation to go out at a later date for coffee.
- I was comfortable/nervous in presenting my business card.
- I was comfortable in ending the conversation and moving on to another.

- I was able to ask some questions that moved the conversation forward.
- Overall I felt less or more nervous in comparison to other networking events.
- What did I learn about myself in this networking situation?

~

USING DEVELOPING BETTER PUBLIC SPEAKING SKILLS AS AN EXAMPLE, WE find new speakers tend to focus on what they see as their shortcomings. Their shortcomings take on a life of their own and minimize the skills and talents that the speaker already has.

Research has shown it is more effective to focus on the skills you already have and strengthen them rather than focus on your own self-defined deficiencies. I believe the same thing applies to networking and conducting 1 to 1 conversations. Find out where your skills are and use them more.

Use the benchmark assessment after each event and reward yourself for areas you have shown improvement, especially those ones that have caused you considerable anxiety in the past.

So what if I do the assessment and I am still having a lot of anxiety? I am really nervous around people.

As I mentioned earlier, shyness can be present in different degrees. Social anxiety can be a problem. I believe managing social situations is a skill that needs to be developed. Like shyness or social anxiety, we are not likely born with well-developed social skills.

Your challenge is to reduce your anxiety to a manageable level. Having worked in the mental health field for over 40 years, often as nurse therapist, I'm not going to make a blanket statement to the effect of "get over it." There can be many causes of anxiety.

While I don't believe in Big Pharma's creating diagnoses such as 'social anxiety' as a new market to sell their medications as a treatment, I do believe if your anxiety appears to be excessive, you really should have a talk with your doctor. There may be other reasons for your anxiety your doctor could help you with. Perhaps a mild antianxiety agent taken before you attend a networking session may help.

If your anxiety is excessive there may be an advantage to you if you were to seek out some help from someone with a psychological background i.e. a psychologist. Sometimes we can use a little help in getting past obstacles we have in life.

I had considered doing so at one point in my life to help me with interpersonal relationships but I chose a self-directed educational program instead. I found one of my challenges was I hadn't developed many of the interpersonal skills at an early age. As an adult I had to go back and learn the basics.

My research exposed me to assertiveness training and communications, conflict/crisis management and systems thinking. As I mentioned earlier about having a tool box, the more skills & techniques you have in your repertoire the less likely you are to become overwhelmed in a situation. If I had to make a single recommendation to anyone as to the secret of leading a successful life I would have to recommend the different areas I researched. It certainly made my life easier.

Another technique I have used in developing my public speaking skills is that of using imagery. Before delivering a presentation to a group or a venue that I'm not used to, I will go up to the front of the room i.e. where I will be delivering the speech from and I will imagine that I am speaking. I will imagine where everyone is seated. I will see their smiling faces and appreciation as to what I am saying. I see myself as being successful.

So when I actually deliver my speech, I have already been successful in my mind. This helps reduce the anxiety I might otherwise experience and allows me to focus on my delivery. The audience quite often doesn't react the same way in reality as they do in my imagination though. Five encores can be a little tiresome!

I believe the same technique can be used prior to participating in a networking event. Imagine yourself being successful, talking to different people and feeling confident.

There is a Law of Attraction principle that addresses creating your own reality. So conversely, if you go to the event with the expectation that you are going to have a stressful time, well then, guess what will happen?

Power Networking Logistics

1. Practice announcing your name out loud.
2. Practice introducing someone else and deliver your introduction out loud.
3. Practice asking questions to another person while you are sharing elevator pitches.
4. During a 1 to 1 conversation with someone, invite them out to coffee.
5. Follow-up with them to set a date & time for the coffee meeting.
6. Ask some colleagues for feedback as to your attire that you are wearing to business networking functions. Is it appropriate and/or how could it be improved?
7. If you don't have a business card, have some printed.
8. Practice presenting and receiving business cards.
9. Purchase and start wearing a name-tag to business networking events.

10. Practice your handshake at home and put it into practice at business networking events.
11. Practice maintaining eye contact in 1 to 1 discussions.
12. Complete the Networking Skills Self-Assessment.

❧

30. POST NETWORKING PHASE

- Follow-up:
- Set up & confirm the coffee meeting
- Research the person on Google & Linkedin
- Knowledge is Power!

K NOWLEDGE IS POWER! - RESEARCH THE PERSON ON GOOGLE & LINKEDIN

As we explored earlier in this book you can easily research the person on-line who you have set up a coffee appointment with. It should be easy to insert their name into Google, or your favourite search engine search box and see what comes up. You are not likely to find the nitty gritty on somebody if that's what you are expecting to find but you will likely find information that can be helpful in learning what their interests and background is.

Another way to research someone is to go to www.pipl.com. They seem to have some internet entries that other sources don't have.

I have found this to be a helpful strategy in several instances. In one case, an individual had been recommended to me as a possible speaker for a panel discussion I was moderating on the topic of bartering.

My research revealed the individual had several past charges for fraud and several more outstanding ones. I saved myself embarrassment by spending a few moments on-line researching.

If you haven't already, Google your own name to see what comes up. Sometimes there are some surprises out there that you may not want to be publicly known, yet it is.

((•)) Power Networking Logistics

1. Follow-up with the person you made contact with to set-up a coffee meeting.
2. Research your coffee meeting partner on Linkedin.
3. Google their name to see what arises.
4. Google your own name.

≈

31. COFFEE'S READY!

- Show up a few minutes early.
- Rule of thumb...
- Don't sell... learn!
- Look for common areas or interest.
- How can you help the other person?
- Develop a servant mind set.

S how up a few minutes early...

Many people experience anxiety over showing up on time for appointments. They fret about the possibility of being late. If you happen to be one, I would suggest arriving a few minutes early. This would likely mean leaving from your current location in a timely manner.

Ensure you have the correct address of the meeting place. I have been caught more than a few times with showing up at the Starbucks that I knew, only to find out that there was another new one a ways down the road. I had to hustle to get there.

Getting there early also allows you to choose a good seat. If you were an undercover operative i.e. secret agent you would also have your back to the wall so that you can see who is coming in as well as having a clear escape route planned. If you're not a spy... well then never mind!

Rule of thumb...

Whoever makes the invitation for coffee pays. But don't count on it! I would suggest you ensure you have enough cash on you or access to debit/credit so you don't get surprised. You wouldn't want to work off a cup of coffee by having to work in the kitchen washing dishes.

Don't sell... learn!

This is your opportunity to learn more about the other person as well as to share your ideas. To learn, you need to ask questions.

Be wary of what I call the bait and switch coffee chat. It starts off with your coffee partner asking about you, what your interests are and seemingly hanging on your every word. They ask you what your aspirations are and what you would like out of life.

Then it's their turn to share. Well guess what? They just happen to have the perfect solution for you. A get rich quick network marketing independent associate position and they jump into a full-fledged multi-media presentation right there in the coffee shop.

I'm not saying that there is anything wrong about network marketing. I believe in it. However, I do not believe in being a captive audience to a sales presentation without having the opportunity to say yay or nay.

Look for common areas of interest.

The intent of this coffee meeting is to explore if there are common areas between the two of you to build a more in depth relationship.

If you have researched your coffee partner, this would be the time to fit these tidbits into conversation. Don't be surprised if they say something to the effect of "You checked me out?" My answer would be "Of course! I check everybody out."

We'll explore looking for common interests in an upcoming chapter.

32. HOW CAN YOU HELP THE OTHER PERSON?

BNI (Business Networking International) has an interesting catch phrase of "Givers Gain!" Develop a servant mind set.

What exactly does that mean? I am not suggesting your role is to wait hand and foot on the other person. Rather, a servant mind set is one where you offer your services and expertise to the other without the expectation of obligation they in turn will provide you something. Nor am I suggesting you work for free or provide free services to them. I am suggesting you offer your expertise or perhaps access to your connections as a way of promoting their business.

If you are a law of attraction believer there is a law of reciprocity. Loosely described it could be "What goes around... comes around." Looking from a positive perspective, if you provide an act of kindness, there is a high chance it will be returned.

I have experienced good returns on creating and submitting testimonials to Linkedin for business colleagues.

Power Networking Logistics

1. Write a list of facts you learned about your coffee partner.
2. Write a list of things you have in common with your coffee partner.
3. What do you have to offer?

∽

33. FOLLOW-UP IS EVERYTHING!

I t can be a great feeling when coming home from a networking event and looking at the stack of business cards you have collected. You even spoke at length to many of the card-donators. Some, it can be a little difficult to recall who they actually were.

"Now was he the tall fellow with the bad hair piece... or was he...?" You've probably experienced that scenario more than once. And you know what... perhaps some of the business people you gave your precious business card to are thinking something similar. Hopefully not about your bad hair though.

For effective business networking I recommend the quality over quantity method. Some would say that networking is a numbers game, the more you meet the higher the chances of your meeting someone who can benefit you. Take for example you are meeting someone for the first time and if the setting and conditions permit, they deliver their elevator pitch and you return with yours. Then comes the awkward moment, what to say next. You can either carry on conversing about something of no consequence "Nice day, eh?" until one of you tires of it or you can explore common interests.

Assuming you have a common interest I would suggest you take the lead in the conversation in getting the other to expand upon the commonality or something they had previously said.

Many networkers make the mistake of trying to sell their product or themselves at the initial meeting. Your goal at that juncture should be to arrange to meet them at another time, perhaps for coffee, to discuss those common areas further.

Even though many of us are electronically connected to our offices by our smart phones and can likely check to see if we are available at a certain date and time to make a coffee date, we likely won't. When you suggest meeting for coffee, later, if the person is willing to set up a date and time, on the spot, I would go with it. Location can always be determined later by e-mail.

If they aren't willing to set a time and date, I would refer to their business card and say something to the effect of "Can I reach you at this e-mail? I'll contact you next week and see if we can set up a time to get together for a quick coffee."

Unfortunately, for many networkers, this is as far as they go. They don't do the follow-up. Life gets busy, there is always one more thing to do with your business and before you know it you have lost the window of opportunity. There is a strong possibility the individual you were networking with also has a list of people they are following up with and other commitments. It is far too easy to get left by the wayside if you don't take action to stand out from the others.

At a morning meeting of a breakfast networking group I belonged to we discussed the issue of follow up. A member related that in his experience, if you actually follow-up with a lead, it puts you way ahead of those that don't. He makes a practice of following up with a networking connection within three days of the original meeting and says it is amazing how many people have said "You know, you are one of the few that actually follows up." Yes, following up can help you stand out from the competition.

The coffee get together is the opportunity for each of you to share your business details and determine if there is enough reason to continue at another time to develop your relationship further and ideally to do business together.

You might ask "I've contacted them three times by e-mail and even left a couple voice mails but they haven't gotten back to me. What do I do next?"

There could be a legitimate reason for them not getting back to you. Life happens! But they could be acting non-assertively and are actively avoiding you. I would have to respond with "If that was true, is that someone that you really want to network with or to do business with?"

If you are to continue it could easily label you as a stalker.

One suggestion may be to add them to your tickler file. A couple weeks down the road, ignoring the fact that they haven't acknowledged you yet, you would be justified in sending them a message something like "I just noticed we didn't get together a few weeks ago like we said we would. Where did the time go? It seems to be picking up speed. Last time we met we were discussing our common interests of... Are you still interested in getting together?" If you still don't receive a response, I would put them in the "inactive" file.

When it comes to networking, to stand out from your competition, remember to follow-up.

$\sim$

34. AN ALTERNATIVE TO LARGE
NETWORKING MEETINGS - A
PLANNED APPROACH

I 've often heard it said in reference to "self-help" books... "If you get only one gem or a useful tip from a book it makes all of your reading time worthwhile." While that may be true, it can have you spending a lot of time with your nose in a book.

The same principal can be applied... inefficiently... to your networking activities... "One contact can make a world of difference in your business..." In essence you are leaving your success to serendipity.

Serendipity, or leaving everything to chance, while awe-inspiring when it works, is not something you can control or count on.

Does the following scenario sound familiar? You attend a large event touted as the best networking event in town. You meet a dozen or so 'new' people, new to you that is, not new to everyone else, or so it would seem.

You deliver your 30-second or longer elevator pitch over the ever-increasing din in the packed room. You go home with a handful of business cards. The next day or so you face the challenge of contacting all of your warm leads. If this is an activity you aren't fond of, that 200-pound phone handset can be quite daunting. "Hi, this is Rae. We met the other night at..."

"Who?"

Okay, perhaps I am injecting my own inadequacies here but I really have heard people agree.

Here is a power networking technique to maximize your effectiveness. If your main purpose in attending a networking event is to get that handful of business cards, then go for it! An alternative option would be meet a business colleague or friend you are comfortable with, in a setting that is conducive to conducting business and compare personal networks. "I'll show you mine... if you show me your's", so to speak. For those that are old enough to recall trading baseball or hockey player cards, this isn't what I am suggesting.

A planned approach is best. For example, I am looking for a book-keeper/accountant to take on a volunteer role in a society that I lead. I would meet with somebody I know who has a background in finances and I could specifically ask them who they would know in their network that might meet my search parameters.

At this preliminary stage it is a matter of brainstorming contact's names. Write them down on a piece of paper. This isn't the time to be evaluating each name as to whether they might be interested in participating, your only task at this point is to generate a list of names.

The idea is to leverage your colleague's network. With social media being so prevalent nowadays, many of us are well connected. Well-connected doesn't mean we actually know or have even met the contact though, more of an e-contact if you will. It probably wouldn't be much of a surprise to find you already know some of the names generated and they are part of your network.

Our next step is to rate each of the names that we have generated as to how well your colleague knows the individual. Would the individual be surprised if you contacted them saying they were referred by your colleague? Or would your contacting the individual trigger a "Who?" response?

Generating a list of names isn't of much use unless you get their accompanying contact info. Now is the time to leverage your connections and make that net work. Make those phone calls.

Don't forget to spend some time helping your colleague with their networking measures. While it can be said "It's not who you know... it's who knows you!", perhaps we need to amend it to "It's not who you know, it's who knows you know who you know!"

~

35. TOP CHARACTERISTICS OF SUCCESSFUL NETWORKERS DERIVED FROM BNI

B NI (Business Networking International) promotes itself as being the largest business network in the world and is founded by Dr. Ivan Misner.

- Having a giving philosophy... givers gain.
- Having a positive attitude. People hate to do business with grumpy people.
- Networking with people that you know. Be a connector.
- Surround yourself with people that are different than you are. They broaden your connections. Factor in different races and culture for diversity.

$\sim$

36. TYPES OF NETWORKERS (DERIVED FROM BNI)

I n one of BNI's podcasts Dr. Misner identified five types of networkers. I want to discuss them at this juncture because it is easy to make generalizations in life. One of them being that everyone else is like we are. It simply isn't true! As you encounter people in your networking activities I would suggest you place them into one of the following categories. You may even come up with your own categories.

Why would we want to you might ask? It can be helpful to understand where somebody is coming from to determine where they are going.

Hermit: Hermits don't have a network, nor do they know how to. They tend to be 'systems' oriented, not a 'people' person. They avoid networking because they don't how to or they are extremely uncomfortable in doing so. They can become more comfortable with training.

Hunter: Hunters are looking for quick sales. They want to 'eat what they kill.' They are not into developing relationships. They are involved in direct sales vs relationship sales. They are not into nurturing a relationship for future sales. I tend to call these ones sharks as they seem to use hit and run as their networking technique. You are only of interest to them until they have made the sale and they move on to the next prey... I mean customer.

Schmoozer: This group is easy to recognize. They seem to have the gift of gab. Socializing and conversing comes easy to them. They really enjoy meeting people. They are often not very good at getting to the next step of developing and nurturing an ongoing relationship. It is far easier to move on to the next exciting conversation.

Apprentice: I would expect many of us reading this book would fall into the category of Apprentice. Meaning we realize our networking skills are in need of improving and we accept the fact they will only improve by practicing them. We are open to making mistakes and learning from them.

Master: The **Master Networker** is what I would imagine we all aspire to be. We would like to have all the skills come second nature to us and be ready, willing and able to take advantage of opportunities as they come our way.

~

37. COMMON FEARS OR BARRIERS EXPERIENCED BY SHY NETWORKERS

Forgetting a Person's Name when they walk up to greet you:
This is often associated with aging but it is probably common at all ages. In a situation where you have a lot on your mind or is emotionally charged for you, it is easy to forget the name of somebody you know quite well.

I find that there are a few causes for this. One example is where you have associated a person with a certain activity or location and then when you see them where you are not expecting to, it becomes easy to doubt yourself. "That can't be....? Sure looks like him though!" I tend to get side-tracked when a woman has changed their hairstyle or hair colouring.

Another is where you have met a person as part of a group introduction and you haven't had a 1 to 1 conversation with them or created the memory patterns of a conversation with them to draw upon. "I know you from somewhere?"

I'm aware of two approaches for this dilemma. One is to just go with the flow. Accept the fact it will happen. Greet the person "Hi there! I must be getting old. I can't remember your name?" or "You look quite familiar to me but I'm drawing a blank. Where do I know you from?"

When they remind me I would laugh at it and carry on with the conversation.

The second approach is a preventative one. It is often suggested when you meet someone for the first time you use the person's name in conversation. "Hello Joe. It's good to meet you." "Well Joe, I have to be going but it was good meeting you." Then it is suggested that you use a memory trick to associate Joe with something that you will recognize. Perhaps Joe drives a Mustang and you could nickname him Mustang Joe.

The secret of course is not calling him by that unless it is a nickname that he actually uses. Some of the memory tricks that we subconsciously use may not be too flattering to the other if we happen to say them out loud.

One way or the other, it isn't the end of the world if you forget somebody's name. It is part of being human.

Asking for Help:

Shy, inexperienced networkers are often reluctant to ask for an individual's assistance because they see networking as an imposition, not an exercise in relationship building. They feel like they are asking someone to do them a favour and also tend to believe they are not worthy of asking the favour. They often try to mitigate their anxiety by apologizing profusely.

This doesn't project a good image for you. Instead, it demonstrates your lack of professionalism and confidence. It's okay to be a little awkward, just don't keep apologizing for it.

The solution to this lays in being assertive. At its basis, assertive behaviour establishes you have as much right as anybody to ask a question or a favour of someone. The challenge is in you believing it.

If you have problems asking for a favour it is likely your internal thought processes are replaying a situation in your life where you had asked a favour and were turned down. Perhaps it created a great deal of embarrassment for you and you vowed never to get in that situation again. Sound familiar? Fear of rejection can be a powerful deterrent to asking for favours.

Like anything else, asking a favour is a skill and skills need to be practiced before you become proficient in using them.

There are different factors to consider before asking a favour that will increase your chances of success.

Factors to consider:

- Is this the right person to ask the favour of?
- Are they likely to be able to grant the favour?
- Will there be a cost to them that might prevent them granting the favour?
- Have they turned your request for a favour down before?
- Is this the right time to ask for this favour?
- What is in it for them?
- Do you have an explanation of why you would like this favour i.e. what would the results be if it was granted?

Nothing to Give Back:

Sometimes shy people have trouble networking because they don't believe they have anything significant, such as a job lead or a contact, to give back to someone who helped them.

While networking and specifically referral networking works better when you do have something to offer, what you have to offer may not be the job lead or a contact. If you show sincere interest in what the other has to say, it is a form of generosity and goes a long way when networking. Being authentic, sharing your passions and offering to help another, can go a long way in advancing your networking efforts.

Tongue-tied:

If you are afraid you will freeze up or get tongue-tied in a social setting, prepare yourself in advance. Think of icebreaker-style questions you can ask. If you are attending a networking event based around a theme, prepare yourself with questions and answers on the theme, so you can offer them without having to put a lot of thought into it at the moment.

Fear of Rejection:

With every interpersonal interaction you encounter, there is the opportunity for rejection. You can't control what the other person is thinking, their motives or whether they decide to help you or not. Don't take it personally and don't dwell on it. They may not be able to help you.

It has become an overused cliché but the word **FEAR**, has been used as an acronym for **False Expectations Appearing Real**. Often our fear is created by our past experiences in similar situations. We are afraid in social situations because we were afraid in the past. It becomes a self-fulfilling prophesy. We need to break the pattern by envisioning being successful in our social interactions.

Being Nervous About Being Nervous:

This is a self-fulfilling prophesy if there ever was one. Another name for it is **anticipatory anxiety**. We are nervous because we expect to be nervous.

Being 'nervous' won't kill you. It is at most a temporary discomfort. As you learn the tips and techniques outlined in this book and actually practice them, your anxiety <u>should</u> reduce.

I say <u>should</u> because everyone is different and skills develop at different speeds. But one thing is for certain, if you don't address your nervousness, it will address you!

What about liquid courage?

Alcohol is known to reduce anxiety in the short term and does disinhibit those that have a problem with inhibitions. You will have to make this decision yourself. As some advertising campaigns have said, "you are your own liquor control board."

$\sim$

PART III

ON-LINE NETWORKING

38. SOCIAL MEDIA OVERVIEW:

S ocial media is here to stay. At least until the next latest and greatest bright shiny objects come along.

Developing an on-line presence and leveraging social media can be a great strategy in reducing your shyness and uncomfortableness with face-to-face networking.

In most cases, your dominant personality traits won't be evident when you are on-line, unless your written language makes it obvious.

A quick on-line search to answer the question "what social media is good for networking?" revealed: Linkedin, Twitter and Instagram as being extraordinary tools for expanding and deepening your connections with business contacts, clients and potential partners.

FIVE TIPS TO NETWORKING THROUGH SOCIAL MEDIA ARE COMMONLY identified:

- Build a social presence
- Post engaging content
- Avoid the hard sell

- Focus on quality over quantity
- Practice good etiquette.

Having been on social media for a while now I agree with the five points. In fact, they seem to be rather self-evident to me.

While I whole-heartedly agree with Linkedin being recognized as a good on-line networking platform, maybe even the best, I don't agree with the suggestion of Twitter and Instagram being used for networking.

The development of different social media platforms and the ability to use them to market products or services has totally changed the face of marketing.

Traditional marketing has had to absorb the new concept of on-line marketing. Many traditional marketers have had to incorporate on-line marketing strategies to stay in business. A plethora of self-proclaimed marketing experts has been the result. Many of them will tell you that you absolutely need to be on social media and they have the skills and time to do it for you. For a fee of course!

Leveraging social media is now within the reach of mere mortals. While I agree that Twitter, Instagram and Facebook for that matter, provide value in promoting yourself, your products and your service, I don't agree with their value in networking.

Sure, you can connect with a lot of people and it looks impressive that you have a massive number of connections but I ask 'are you really networking?'

I question the value of these connections. Twitter has evolved into a one-way data dump where everybody is pushing their content. As for meaningful conversations on Twitter, as far as I'm concerned... it's a joke.

I think Facebook is a great place to promote yourself however, I have many 'best friends' I have never met and am not likely to.

I'm sure there are a lot of social media enthusiasts who will disagree with me. In light of our subject for discussion being 'power networking', I think you would be better off investing your time and energy in different places.

Power networking is about leveraging strategies to make you a better networker.

IN THE NEXT CHAPTER WE DIG INTO USING LINKEDIN TO DEVELOP YOUR network. This will be time well spent as one of your power networking strategies. It has for me.

～

39. ARE YOU LINKEDIN?

A re you Linkedin? Well you should be!

Linkedin and the internet in general are a boon to shy networkers. The on-line world is a great leveler when it comes to the shy and introverted vs. the extroverted. When you are reading text on a website or elsewhere, the personality of the author doesn't usually show. I believe many introverts have better computer and technological skills than our extroverted colleagues. I believe our ability to focus on matters and our preference to work alone works in our favour.

You can research a person you want to connect to without ever having to leave the comfort of your home. Mobile apps on your smart phone also mean you can research somebody when you are out and about. You don't have to wait until you are in front of your desktop computer of laptop for that matter.

I used to describe Linkedin as being like your resume on steroids. The content I had uploaded to my profile was very much in the curriculum vitae style of a resume. It seemed to go on and on when you were reading it. I had added every notable achievement to my list of accomplishments. The fact I was involved with and had lots of experience from many different organizations as well as my professional career as a Registered Nurse, made it confusing.

There are seven elements of Linkedin I want to focus on in this section that are helpful to a shy networker.

YOUR PERSONAL MARKETING AGENCY:

One of the first steps to take after opening your Linkedin account is to start to develop your **Profile**. Your profile connects you with others in your Linkedin network. As a new connection is made, often the new contact will go to your profile to learn more about you. Even people you have known for years will check you out. Imagine the number one thought going through someone's mind as they read your profile is... "Is there an opportunity for me to do business with this person?"

PARTS OF THE PROFILE:

Your Name: You have the option of having your name displayed fully or with your first name and last initial. Example: Rae Stonehouse vs Rae S. If you are using Linkedin as a business growth strategy it is suggested you use your full name.

Headline: Provide a descriptive headline statement. It does not need to be your current job title, although many people use this field in that way. Something that gives a glimpse into your uniqueness or personality can help you stand out from your competitors.

Rae Stonehouse DTM aka Mr. EMCEE
Master Organizer: I make things happen!
Kelowna, British Columbia, Canada · Events Services

Mr. Emcee: Okanagan Valley Entrepreneur Society (OVES)
Okanagan Help 4 Biz
Toastmasters, District 21

Edit Profile ·   500+

ca.linkedin.com/in/raestonehouse/   Contact Info

In the **Background** heading you can add a **Summary** of your experience and what you currently have to offer. Under **Experience** you can add any experience you want highlighted. This is a good place to highlight your strengths and accomplishments. You can add bulleted points in this section, but it should not be all bullet points. Write your summary as if you are speaking conversationally to the person reading it.

It might be helpful to take a look at some other Linkedin user profiles to see how they have completed their profile. Every connection you gain won't necessarily be a business prospect for you. However, as you write your profile, you should do so with the intent a prospect will read it.

This is the place to blow your own horn! Make sure you highlight what you want the reader to see and to remember. Some people take a factual or chronological approach to creating their profile, others, more of a promotional or marketing one. My original profile included references to my nursing career and was designed for the possibility of using it for job search purposes. As I am approaching the end of my nursing career and moving into other ventures I have removed references to my profession in favour of my entrepreneurial ventures and my volunteer life.

HERE ARE SOME GENERAL TIPS:

- Capitalize properly. "mary smith" is less professional than "Mary Smith."
- Proofread, proofread, proofread
- Avoid industry jargon as much as possible
- Avoid acronyms. If you must use them, explain the acronym in the first appearance of it in your profile. Example: ASAP (as soon as possible)
- Use a professional headshot photo of yourself for your profile. More about that later.

An earlier version of my Linkedin profile (see below) was written tongue-in-cheek. It had the following opening sentences:

<<How many people can honestly say that they spent part of their formative years in a maximum security hospital for the criminally insane?

Rae can! True, he was working as a staff in the Dietary Department and was able to go home every evening at the end of his shift but that experience has had a lasting effect on him.

Over the past 30+ years Rae has been working as a Registered Nurse, predominantly in the field of mental health/psychiatric nursing.>>

BACKGROUND

SUMMARY

How many people can honestly say that they spent part of their formative years in a maximum security hospital for the criminally insane?

Rae can! True, he was working as a staff in the Dietary Department and was able to go home every evening at the end of his shift but that experience has had a lasting effect on him.

Over the past 30+ years Rae has been working as a Registered Nurse, predominantly in the field of mental health/psychiatric nursing.

Rae is driven by the creative process. He is passionate about turning ideas into reality. His time in Toastmasters has shown him that our personal limitations are really only our own inhibitions. Rae has learned to move beyond his comfort zone and possibly more inhibitions than the average person and make things happen! Attitude = Altitude! Ask him how he can help turn your idea into reality.

As a social entrepreneur, he is leading the Okanagan Valley Entrepreneurs Society to becoming a valuable resource for fellow entrepreneurs.

In this version I have taken a promotional approach many would find uncomfortable in using. It doesn't seem to have held me back any for those who have wanted to connect with me.

Currently I am using a more formalized profile overview, yet still promotional in nature.

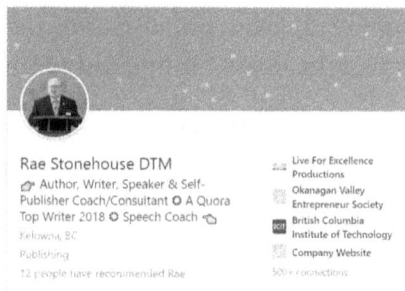

Rae Stonehouse DTM
Author, Writer, Speaker & Self-Publisher Coach/Consultant O A Quora Top Writer 2018 O Speech Coach
Kelowna, BC
Publishing
12 people have recommended Rae

Live For Excellence Productions
Okanagan Valley Entrepreneur Society
British Columbia Institute of Technology
Company Website
500+ connections

RAE A. STONEHOUSE IS A CANADIAN BORN AUTHOR & SPEAKER.

His professional career as a Registered Nurse working predominantly in psychiatry/mental health, has spanned four decades.

Rae has embraced the principal of CANI (Constant and Never-ending Improvement) as promoted by thought leaders such as Tony Robbins and brings that philosophy to each of his publications and presentations.

Rae has dedicated the latter segment of his journey through life to overcoming his personal inhibitions. As a 25+ year member of Toastmasters International he has systematically built his self-confidence and communicating ability.

He is passionate about sharing his lessons with his readers and listeners. His publications thus far are of the self-help, self-improvement genre and systematically offer valuable sage advice on a specific topic.

His writing style can be described as being conversational. As an author Rae strives to have a one-to-one conversation with each of his readers, very much like having your own personal self-development coach.

Rae is known for having a wry sense of humour that features in his publications.

To learn more about Rae A. Stonehouse, visit the Wonderful World of Rae Stonehouse at http://raestonehouse.com or 250-451-6564

Specialties:

➤ Author of self-help books & on-line courses

➤ Speech presentation coaching & training

➤ Communicating & leadership skill development

➤ Keynote, workshop, seminar presenting & writing

➤ Facilitating/group moderating

➤ Website development & maintenance (Joomla & Wordpress)

➤ Recognized as a Top Writer 2018 at Quora for over 700 answers & 750,000 answer views

ANOTHER FEATURE TO ADD TO YOUR PROFILE IS **HONOURS & AWARDS**. If you have some and they are related to your profession or business venture, this is the place to promote them. I wouldn't recommend listing your first place bowling trophy unless you happen to be a professional bowler and you wanted people to be aware of the fact.

You can also promote **Publications** you have created and/or published as well as websites you have created or are associated with.

As you build your network you can solicit **Recommendations** from people you have assisted in some capacity or conducted business with. These are testimonials that can prove to be quite powerful in helping someone who has come upon your name when they have been researching a specific search term in making a decision to contact you or not. You in turn, can provide recommendations for others you have worked with.

As you build your network it is worth your while to provide testimonials for other Linkedin members you have worked with, assuming you have something positive to say about them of course! The Law of Reciprocity often kicks in when you do so. When you submit a recommendation that has been unsolicited by another, they often feel obligated and create and submit a testimonial on your behalf in return.

Skills & Endorsements is a category Linkedin seems to believe has great value. I believe it would work against you if you didn't have anything in this area however, as to whether it benefits you in any way, I don't think so.

Whereas **Recommendations** requires some thought by the contributor, the **Skills & Endorsements** only require a click by the endorser. I've been highly recommended by connections I have never met and am unlikely to ever meet. Where is the value... or the credibility for that matter of these endorsements?

With a little bit of work you can create a Linkedin profile that grabs the interest of the reader and has a higher chance of creating an opportunity. Something to remember is the search engines will not only index and post your Linkedin profile, but it will often link you with everyone you are linked to.

For example, if a person is searching for someone you are linked to and they have used their name as the search criteria, there is a high chance your name will appear in the search results for the other person. Your chances of being found in the search engines increase even more if you have chosen your keywords in your personal profile carefully.

So why bother doing this much work? A big part of networking is being visible. If people don't know you, they won't likely do business with you. As an event planner working with small business owners and entrepreneurs I used the Linkedin Search feature quite frequently to target my search for whatever field or profession I was looking for.

When I am invited by somebody to connect with them in Linkedin the first things I check out is their photo, their profile and the number of people they have connected to.

I tend to be suspicious when I see only a small amount of content posted under their Profile. Either they are just starting to create their profile, they are too lazy to upload the content, they really don't buy into the concept of sharing personal info on Linkedin or perhaps they are paranoid and don't want to share anything. Could be any of those reasons but I as the visitor to your site shouldn't have to jump to conclusions as to why you don't have much content posted.

Another area I find problematic is the photos that people post of themselves. Your photo is an extension of your personal or business marketing plan. Save the cutesy photos of your dog or a close up of your eye or nose for Facebook. In fact posting a logo or a picture of your pet could get you kicked off of Linkedin as it is against the rules and is listed in their terms of reference. I want to see what the person looks like if I am going to consider working with them.

As children, we were advised not to judge a book by its cover. Yet, we do it all the time. You only have about two to three seconds to make a good first impression with someone checking out your profile with the possibility of doing business with you. Do you really want to waste that opportunity?

IT CAN BE YOUR PERSONAL RESEARCH DEPARTMENT:

Once your profile is posted you are able to start connecting with other members.

You can also research a person you want to connect to without ever having to leave the comfort of your home. Mobile apps on your smart phone also mean you can research somebody when you are out and about. You don't have to wait until you are in front of your desktop computer.

The Basic Linkedin package anyone can get for free includes a few features that can aid your research.

YOU CAN SEARCH FOR PEOPLE, JOBS, COMPANIES, BY INSERTING TEXT INTO the text box and clicking on the Add new search icon graphic.

Linkedin originally had a feature that allowed you to do an Advanced Search. With their moving to a revenue-raising model, sadly this is no longer available for free. You can still access it however, as the saying goes "it'll cost you!"

An additional search technique is to search for the individual through your favourite search engine. Linkedin and Facebook profiles seem to get indexed quite readily. With many people sharing the same name, ensure that you have the identified the correct person.

40. REACH OUT AND LINK
SOMEBODY

A network is composed of more than one person. If you don't reach out and invite somebody to connect, or you don't receive any invitations to connect, then you don't really have a network.

Sending out an invitation to another Linkedin member can be a challenge for many shy people. We can tend to second guess ourselves... "Why would anyone want to connect with me?"

The Linkedin program will automatically send you notifications of people you might know and ask you whether you would like to connect with them. This can be a double-edged sword as the saying goes. On one side, if you are connected with somebody, Linkedin will send you a list of names of people they are connected to and ask you if you would like to invite them to connect. If the names presented are people you know already and they would know you, by all means send them an invitation to connect.

The other edge of the sword comes into play when you submit an invitation to somebody you know and they respond to the invitation with the answer they don't know you. A few years back, while using the Linkedin app on my Iphone, I was sending out numerous invitations to connect with people who I thought would recognize my name only to find that Linkedin decided to punish me.

Apparently if too many people say they don't recognize you it triggers something in the system that takes away your privilege to send out an invitation to people you are connected with. At the time, while seemingly being punished for what Linkedin encouraged me to do, I had the extra step of having to add the individual's e-mail address as part of my invitation to connect.

Here is a list of tips to prevent restrictions from the Linkedin site:

- Invite only people that you personally know.
- Invite only those you'd recommend to others.
- Personalize your invitation message. Explain how you know them or why you want to connect.
- Add a current head-shot photo to your profile so people recognize you.
- Use an InMail or Introduction if you don't know someone's email address. (these are currently paid features)
- Use the **Ignore** button for invitations from someone you know but choose not to connect with.
- Only use the <u>I Don't Know</u> option when you truly don't know the member.

~

41. SEND MESSAGES OUT:

L inkedin has added the sending e-mail out feature to several of their paid subscriptions.

However, there is limited ability in the free subscription to send out a message to members of groups you belong to.

You can send a message to a group member without being connected and adjust your **Member Message** settings from within the group.

To send a free message to a group member:

1. Click **Groups** at the top of your home page.
2. Click the group's name.
3. Click the **Members** tab.
4. Move your cursor over the member's name and click the **Send message** link revealed on the right.
5. This link will appear if the member's settings allow them to be contacted by other group members.
6. Create your message and click **Send Message**.

Note: You can also click on a member's picture from the **Discussions** page and then click **Message.**

To view or adjust your **Member Messages** settings:

1. Click **Groups** at the top of your home page.
2. Click the group's name.
3. Click the group's **...** tab.
4. Click **Update Your Settings**.
5. Next to **Messaging**, check or uncheck the box next to choose whether group members in your extended network can message you.

Note: Contact information isn't shared when you use the **Send message** link though groups. Messages they send on your behalf only show the name on your account.

42. CREATE A DATABASE OF CONTACTS AND CONTACT INFO

I suggested in the last chapter that you keep a database of your Linkedin connections.

While this process is extra work for you, there is value in saving your contact list on a regular basis. At any time you could run amok of your Linkedin Terms of Service and lose access to your contacts.

Backing up your list won't provide you with the rich content you can discover about a connection however, you will at least have their contact info.

You can export a list of the connections you have made on LinkedIn at any time.

From Linkedin:

To export LinkedIn connections:

CLICK THE ME ICON AT THE TOP OF YOUR LINKEDIN HOMEPAGE.

Select **Settings & Privacy** from the dropdown.

Click the **Privacy** tab at the top of the page.

Under the **How LinkedIn uses your data section,** click **Change** next to **Download your data.**

Note: You may be prompted to sign in.

You'll be redirected to the **Download your data page** where you can select **Connections.**

You will receive an email to your Primary Email address which will include a link where you can download your list of connections.

The CSV and vCard formats don't support all characters. As a result, languages with extended character sets, such as Chinese, Japanese, or Hebrew are not supported.

You currently can't export a list of your contacts that are not 1st-degree connections.

If you're exporting your connections because you have a duplicate account, remember to:

Close your extra account.

Import your connections list to another LinkedIn account, make sure you've saved the file in a location you can find, and then follow the instructions for uploading contacts using a CSV file.

When you receive your e-mail from Linkedin you can download it to your computer and then open it with Excel. The downside is only the **full name, email address, current employer, and position** are exported.

You will need to manually access each of your contact's profiles on Linkedin to see if their phone number or mailing address is posted. If so, with a lot of work, you can easily collect the data and add it to your new contact spreadsheet. Be sure to save the spreadsheet with a name you will easily recognize. I change the date on my spreadsheets every time I update so I always have a backup copy should something happen to the one I am currently working on.

43. SYSTEMATIZE RESPONDING TO
NEW CONNECTIONS

A s you build your database of contacts it is worthwhile sending the new contact a brief message outlining who you are, what you are up to right now and open the door for future possibilities which would include meeting in person.

It has been my experience very few people actually do so. And by doing so, you will stand out from the crowd. For a shy networker this can have the advantage of promoting yourself without increasing your anxiety level.

A few years back I was the Chair of a local entrepreneur's society. I also cared for their social media presence with Facebook and a Linkedin groups. My goal at the time was to be one of the most connected people to the local business world.

As Linkedin members would ask to join the society's Linkedin group, I would assess their suitability for the group and I would also send them back an invitation to join my business and professional network on Linkedin and in the real world.

Utilizing an invitation to connect template i.e. a letter I had created and saved, I sent it out to over 800 Linkedin members who were local business professionals and might be interested in what I had to offer.

As for people I meet at local networking events, if there is a common interest or bond, I will usually connect with them over the next few days. For these individuals I likely wouldn't send them the template message I mentioned above.

If I have met with someone already or had business dealings with them I would likely adapt the text on the template to refer to our past experience together and target what I am promoting to their interests.

∽

44. PARTICIPATE IN GROUPS

Linkedln Groups provide a place for professionals in the same industry or with similar interests to share content, find answers, post and view jobs, make business contacts, and establish themselves as industry experts. Joining a group is a good way to increase your network of connections. Some groups are private to the members only, so only the members would see your posts. Other groups that are public would allow your posts to be seen by anyone.

You can find groups to join in the **Groups Directory** or view suggestions of groups you may like. You can also create a new group focused on a particular topic or industry.

Finding a group you want to join:

1. Move your cursor over **Groups** at the top of your homepage, and select **Groups Directory** from the dropdown menu.
2. Browse the **Featured Groups** on the page.
3. Search for a group using the **Search Groups** box on the left.
4. Move your cursor over **Groups** at the top of your homepage and select **Groups You May Like** from the dropdown menu.
5. Browse through their list of suggested groups.

Choosing the right group for you:

You can get more details about a group and find out if people in your network are members on the **Group Profile** page.

1. Click a group's name to view its **Discussions** page.
2. Click the **More...** tab under the group's name and select **Group Profile.**

Joining a group:

- Click **Join Group** on the group **Discussions** page or anywhere you see the button.

OR

- Respond to an invitation from a group member or manager.

SOMETHING TO KEEP IN MIND IS THERE ARE TWO KINDS OF GROUPS: closed and open. When you post to an open group, your comments will appear in the Updates section for all of your connections to view. If this is desirable, then this works for you. If you are posting something you assumed was private or confidential to a specific group, it may be problematic. Rule of thumb is to not post anything that could come back to haunt you.

If you don't see a group that meets your needs, consider creating your own. You can belong to up to 50 groups and own 10.

I am the Owner of a Linkedin group for a non-profit society for entrepreneurs that I was also the Chairman of the Board. The group is closed to members and you have to ask to join it. I try to limit membership to local business people, entrepreneurs and professionals. As this is my target market for my business as well, it serves as source of new connections for me.

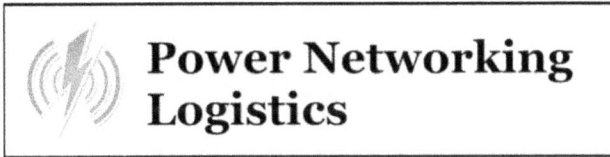

Power Networking Logistics

1. Develop and upload your Linkedin profile.
2. Create your headline.
3. Create a Summary of what you have to offer.
4. Add a professional head-shot photo of yourself.
5. Add your Honors & Awards.
6. Add your Publications if you have any. Don't forget to add a link.
7. Ask for recommendations from people that you have worked with.
8. Provide recommendations for people that you have worked with.
9. Send invitations to connect to people that you know and would likely know you.
10. Accept invitations from others to connect.
11. Develop a template to send to Linkedin connections that thanks them after connecting with you and introduces yourself to them and opens the door for further connection.
12. Create a Powerpoint presentation for the Slideshare application and add to your profile.
13. Start monitoring the Update feature. Post your own updates or comment on others.
14. Send messages to your connections through Linkedin.
15. Search for groups that you are interested in and/or that would allow you to be visible in. Participate in these groups on a regular basis.
16. Create a database of contacts.

45. BLOW YOUR OWN HORN!

I 've mentioned it a few times already in this book. To be successful in business you need to be able to self-promote... blow your own horn so to speak. The same applies in being a successful networker. If you are researching others, likely they are researching you as well. Make sure you give them something to remember you by.

If you are providing a service or a product that others do as well, you will need to try to stand out from the crowd. Linkedin Basic includes **Slide Share** which allows you to upload a Powerpoint Presentation to www.slideshare.net and have it be accessible on your Profile. It can be a great way to promote yourself and your product or service.

The **newsfeed** section of your profile gives you up to date notifications from those you are connected to. Ask a question, share a thought or post an article. This feature can be a good way to send out announcements about special projects you are involved with or to promote something of importance to you. If you have a blog and you have just released the latest edition, promote it here. While it is possible to do, resist the urge to have your Facebook and Twitter account automatically post your content to Linkedin. Each of these three social media venues has their advantages but what works in one might not in the other.

The **newsfeed** is also a great way to keep tabs on the interests of people you may be considering networking with. With each post you have the opportunity to **Like**, **Share** or **Comment**. This can be a good way to start an on-line relationship. It can make it easier for you if and when you actually meet this connection in person. You will already have something in common and can build on it from there.

Sharing your accomplishments will help you find opportunities to teach others, which is part of the process of networking. Be proud of all your accomplishments, whether they seem small, large, significant, easy or difficult. Allow your natural talents & abilities to be the gift you give to your network.

The concept of 'blowing your own horn' may be difficult for some people. Many of us have been taught that talking about yourself is bragging. I believe that it was Walt Whitman who said "If you done it, it ain't bragging!" A technique that works well at removing that illusion of bragging is to submit an update that focuses on someone else.

An example could be "I would like to thank XXX for inviting me to speak at their recent conference on my favourite topic of Conflict Resolution!"

If XXX is a member of Linkedin, the message will show up on their Updates as well as yours. So on one hand you are thanking the other person, who will likely appreciate being recognized publicly, but it will also draw attention to your name and whatever you are trying to draw attention to. In this example, I am focusing on speaking about conflict resolution. This falls into a 'win-win' situation and would increase the likelihood might research the fact I present seminars on conflict resolution.

~

46. CYBER BULLYING PREVENTION STRATEGIES

I f you are actively marketing and promoting yourself on-line as a part of your networking efforts the likelihood of encountering a cyber bully increases exponentially. It is simply a matter of numbers, the more people you network with the higher the odds of encountering one.

Cyber bullying has featured prominently lately in the media with the unfortunate suicides of several teens in North America. As adults we aren't immune to the same tactics these bullies use.

SO WHAT IS A "CYBERBULLY"?

FROM WIKIPEDIA, THE FREE ENCYCLOPEDIA...CYBERBULLYING IS THE USE of the Internet and related technologies to harm other people, in a deliberate, repeated, and hostile manner.

Cyberbullying is defined in legal glossaries as:

- actions that use information and communication technologies to support deliberate, repeated, and hostile behavior by an individual or group, that is intended to harm another or others.

- use of communication technologies for the intention of harming another person
- use of internet service and mobile technologies such as web pages and discussion groups as well as instant messaging or SMS text messaging with the intention of harming another person.

Examples of what constitutes cyberbullying include communications that seek to intimidate, control, manipulate, put down, falsely discredit, or humiliate the recipient. The actions are deliberate, repeated, and hostile behaviour intended to harm another. Cyberbullying has been defined by The National Crime Prevention Council: "When the Internet, cell phones or other devices are used to send or post text or images intended to hurt or embarrass another person."

The practice of cyberbullying is not limited to children and, while the behaviour is identified by the same definition when practiced by adults, the distinction in age groups sometimes refers to the abuse as cyberstalking or cyberharassment when perpetrated by adults toward adults.

Common tactics used by cyberstalkers are performed in public forums, social media or online information sites and are intended to threaten a victim's earnings, employment, reputation, or safety. Behaviours may include encouraging others to harass the victim and trying to affect a victim's on-line participation. Many cyberstalkers try to damage the reputation of their victim and turn other people against them. **Source:** Wikipedia... Cyberbullying & Cyberstalking.

A cyberbully could be a complete stranger to you or someone you know.

This article is a result of having dealt with a cyberbully over a period of five months, one that I have never actually met in person. I would like to share some cyberbullying prevention strategies that I have learned during my journey so you don't have to go through the misery. And that dear reader is what the bully wants. They want you to be miserable. Your misery is their goal.

My experience began innocently enough when I cautioned a poster to a Facebook Group page I moderated. The individual had added their comments to a post I had made and side-tracked the conversation. As the Moderator I felt the content posted was inappropriate for a public forum as it was harassing another member of the group and making veiled threats.

I advised the individual firstly, I felt that the content they posted was inappropriate for a public forum. Secondly, their dispute was with an individual and that they should deal with them directly. Thirdly, I made myself available for discussion of this matter and should they continue further in this manner I would be obligated to revoke their membership from the Facebook group.

In their self-righteous indignation they quickly posted several more posts, however this time they were directed at me. As I had previously cautioned them I revoked their membership to the group page, which in turn deleted the comments to the post.

Thinking the incident was over I was dismayed to find a tirade of accusations posted on their Twitter feed about me. I then found I was highlighted on their website's blog as being the scourge of mankind as well as attacked on their personal Facebook page. I like attention as much as the next guy but this was out of control!

The intent of this article is not to get into the "he said"... "she said" details of this situation but to learn from it.

I had worked some 33 years as a Registered Nurse in the field of psychiatry/mental health and through those years I believe that I have developed a good understanding of human behaviour. At least I am able to recognize behaviour that does not fall within the parameters of so-called normal behaviour. Over the next few paragraphs I will endeavour to provide some background info on why bullies bully from a psychological perspective. It isn't a one size fits all profile but I would challenge you to think about people you know or have encountered and determine if they fall into any of these categories.

Some people display paranoid personality traits without meeting all of the criteria of being diagnosed as a paranoid personality disorder. Common characteristics of a paranoid individual are as follows: suspiciousness (looking for hidden reasons, meanings, causes etc. to another's behaviour and/or actions); hypervigilance i.e. being super aware of situations that they feel could cause them harm; short-tempered and lack of trust. The individual that is bullying you may have paranoia and for whatever reasons have chosen you as a target.

Working in mental health for so many years I learned an adage that has served me well... 'all behaviour has meaning.' The challenge is in determining what the meaning of the behaviour is and what it is supposed to do for the individual displaying it.

A cyberbully displays the same characteristics of a bully in the "real world." They usually have inadequate personalities, poor interper-sonal skills, poor coping skills and a lack of empathy. They seek out individuals who they feel that by dominating them, they can raise their stature.

I recall a book written back in the 1970's entitled The Games People Play, by a psychologist named Eric Berne. Berne outlined different interpersonal transactions that people have with each other calling them "games". Ideally, as adults respectful of each other, we commu-nicate at the same level and the communication is productive.

Another game, one that is not productive is "I'm not okay, you're okay!" In this game one person does not feel good about themselves. They have learned that if they bring another person i.e. one who is okay, down to their level they subsequently feel better about them-selves. It is definitely dysfunctional but it is a game that is likely fairly common. A bully looks at another person and decides that they want to bring them down to their level. Victims are created. Victims may not even know in the beginning that they have been targeted or why. Victims are not always passive individuals who are setting themselves up for bullying as some people would believe. A bully may target an individual who is more popular, attractive, successful, charismatic, smarter etc. than they believe they are.

This article is focusing on the on-line behaviour of a bully, also known as cyberbullying. Perhaps you will encounter them on a Facebook page as I did or any of the numerous discussion groups that proliferate on the internet.

For whatever reason, you are chosen as their target. It might start out with their disagreement of something you have posted. Then it escalates to attacking not only your content but your credibility in posting the comments. Then it becomes a personal attack where your personal traits and characteristics and so-called short comings are focused on. It doesn't matter what you respond with as the bully's focus is in maintaining one-up-manship, thereby controlling you.

You can tell that you are dealing with a paranoid individual in that they will likely respond to your post in a matter of minutes. They are at the ready, waiting for your response to be posted and then with a distant "Gotcha!" they respond back in a caustic manner. "How dare you!" seems to be their battle cry.

Cyberbullies will often align themselves with influential people or organizations, where there may not be an actual connection, in order to add credence to their accusations. They will often make generalizing statements. "Everyone says that you...!" "XXX agrees with me that you..." "You always..."

So what can you do to mitigate the damage done by a cyberbully? As William Feathers is often quoted as saying "knowledge is power!" You need to regain your power from the bully and mitigate the damage they can do to you. Something to remember is anything posted to the internet will likely be there forever. If you are in business and trying to develop a business or personal brand via networking and/or using the internet it is important to think of damage control.

The following is a list of strategies you can use to regain your power over a cyberbully. They are not organized in steps but rather initiatives that can be underway at the same time.

SOCIAL MEDIA DISCUSSION GROUPS:

If one of your posts is targeted by a bully, as hard as it will be, you need to resist the urge to respond in kind. This is what the bully wants. By responding, in their mind you justify what they wrote and that gives them the impetus to continue and escalate their postings. It takes at least two people to argue. If you don't, it makes it more challenging for them to continue on their own.

If you are the Moderator of the group and you are under attack from a bully I would suggest responding to them with a firm directive approach as used in the human resources field. Provide them with an explanation of what behaviour is inappropriate, what behaviour would be appropriate and/or corrective measures you would suggest to improve the situation, a time frame for the changes to take place and finally an outline of what measures you will take if the inappropriate behaviour is not corrected. If the behaviour continues, follow through with the measures you had outlined.

It is difficult to determine how the cyberbully will respond with the above described actions. It could escalate matters. It is also difficult if not impossible to predict the future and the past can get blurry as matters escalate. I would recommend you create a document in your favourite word processing program to chronicle the steps you have taken in the matter and to provide evidence of the abuse that has been directed your way. I would recommend an inexpensive program called Snagit from Techsmith. It allows you to do screen captures of info that you want to keep. Simply highlight an area you want to capture. It loads it into the Snagit editor where you can copy and paste into your word document.

If at anytime you feel that your personal safety is at risk, notify your local police department. In my case, I sought out legal advice and was advised to take out a peace bond on the individual. This is a legal document that you can present to the police should a person be within your immediate vicinity without just cause. My local police declined following up on my complaint saying the individual hadn't crossed over from being a nuisance to an actual threat and they were seeing an increase in this type of behaviour. Since I wasn't able to get a peace bond secured, I did ensure a file was initiated at the police detachment and my details were recorded should I need to refer to them at a later date. This was all added to my personal file.

If you are the creator of the post the bully has used as a soapbox you are likely able to delete the entire post. This takes it away from public view. The downside of this action is that should you do so, you will be unable to register a complaint with the Administrators of the specific social media. Once it is deleted, it is gone. Forever? I'm not sure about that. Make sure you do a screen shot capture before deleting the entries. We will explore how to register a complaint shortly.

FACEBOOK:

IF THE POST IN QUESTION I.E. WHERE YOU HAVE BEEN ATTACKED IS created by someone else you can report it to Facebook administration by clicking on the small ... that appears in the top right hand corner of the original post. It gives you the option of reporting the post or labeling it as spam. Doing so takes the post out of the Timeline and presumably Facebook will investigate it. If you are the originator of the post you only have the option of hiding your post or deleting it. Remember to take a screen capture before taking action.

· · ·

TWITTER:

TWITTER SEEMS TO BE A LITTLE MORE OUT FRONT WITH HOW THEY process complaints "Users are allowed to post content, including potentially inflammatory content, provided they do not violate the Twitter Rules and Terms of Service."

"In order to investigate reports of abusive behaviors, violent threats or a breach of privacy, we need to be in contact with the actual person affected or their authorized representative. We are unable to respond to requests from uninvolved parties regarding those issues to mitigate the likelihood of false or unauthorized reports. If you are not an authorized representative but you are in contact with the individual, encourage the individual to file a report through our forms."

You can also unfollow a person who is harassing you on Twitter. This removes them from your timeline but not from the Twitter stream. Their posts will remain visible on their Twitter profile homepage. Remember to take a screen capture before unfollowing them.

LINKEDIN:

LINKEDIN DOESN'T SEEM TO ADDRESS THE ISSUE OF ABUSIVE POSTS other than advising that you can report inappropriate comments by flagging a group discussion.

"Open the discussion and click Flag to notify the group manager that an item might be inappropriate, or that it may need to be moved to the Jobs or Promotions tab.

To flag a comment in a group discussion:

Move your cursor over a comment and click Flag as inappropriate under a comment.

You can also contact your group owner or manager directly. The group manager decides what action (if any) will be taken.

WEBSITE OR BLOG:

IF MALICIOUS CONTENT IS BEING POSTED ABOUT YOU ON THE cyberbully's website or blog an option is to register a complaint with their webhosting provider and or their website developer. This information is generally available by doing a Whois domain lookup in a search engine such as Google. In my case, the website developer tried to mitigate his responsibility by saying that he wasn't responsible for the content of the site only the operating system. I left him with the idea that he may share liability should I decide to go forward with legal proceedings against the cyberbully.

Speaking of Google... it is worth your while to Google yourself every so often to see what is floating around in cyberspace about you. Simply enter your name into Google or another search engine to see what is out there. When your results are displayed Google allows you to fine tune your search. Simply click on Search Tools and you indicate the time span that you would like displayed.

IN SUMMARY, CYBERBULLYS CAN MAKE YOUR LIFE MISERABLE AND TAKE your concentration away from more important issues, if you let them. To be successful at networking you need to open yourself up to possibilities and unfortunately one of those possibilities is that someone will want to take advantage of you or do harm. I hope that this article will give you strategies to regain your power should you encounter a cyberbully. Bullying in any form should not be tolerated and we all need to do our part to reduce it. Please share this article with anyone that you feel may benefit.

47. TOP 15 NETWORKING NO-NO'S

Throughout this book and my other publications I have provided tips & techniques to help improve your networking effectiveness. I thought it would be interesting and perhaps entertaining to take a look at the subject from a different perspective i.e. what you really <u>shouldn't</u> do.

These aren't provided in any order of priority. See if you recognize any of them from your adventures in networking land.

1. **No Show: (Not showing up for an appointment)** When all is said and done it can be argued that all you really own in life is your reputation. There are some people who don't respect other people's time. They make appointments they don't intend to keep, or they pre-empt the appointment for something more important than meeting with you. Soon they get the reputation of not being reliable or keeping commitments. Is this the reputation you want to develop?
2. **No Follow-up: (Not following up on something that you said that you would do)** BNI (Business Network International) founder Dr. Ivan Misner promotes the concept of 'givers gain.' Offering to help someone with

something or providing information that can help an individual move their business forward without expecting compensation is a good way to develop a network connection. Not following-up on what you said you were going to do takes away from your credibility and your reputation.

3. **No Follow-up: (Not following through with contacting a connection)** If you say you are going to follow-up with someone... do so. If you don't, at the least, you have missed an opportunity to develop a potential profitable connection. At the worst, well who knows! See **Follow-up is Everything!** for an expanded version of why you should follow-up.

4. **Not focusing on your conversation partner i.e. looking around the room for a better offer.** I think we are guilty of this at one time or another. Let's face it, not everybody is interesting to listen to. And you know what... our conversation partner might be thinking the same thing about us! Listening is a skill. You will find the more you listen to people, the more they think you are interested in them, the more they will reveal about themselves and they will think you are a fantastic conversationalist.

5. **Sexist or racist language.** I hear this far too often in conversations with people that should know better. It isn't acceptable and I don't want to hear it.

6. **Fly undone!** Gents for heaven's sake check your fly when you leave the restroom. It might be a great conversation starter "So the bull's ready to get out is it?" But is this where you want the conversation to go? It can be challenging to recover from a position of embarrassment. Trust me I know. I was on stage for two hours once as an emcee with my fly undone.

7. **I'm so wonderful! (Going on and on about yourself and not giving the other person a chance to talk)** If you have been on the receiving end of listening to one of these types you

will know it is not fun. I would suggest hitting the Pause button and move on to the next opportunity.

8. **Talking about someone else i.e. a third party who isn't part of the conversation in a derogatory manner.** Some people are happiest when they are putting somebody else down. If you participate with someone like this, you are validating their behaviour and you will likely soon be labeled the same way. This is basically gossip. And you can almost guarantee if they are telling you something juicy about someone else, they are sharing tidbits about you too.

9. **Dump job: (Using your conversational partner as a sounding board without asking their permission to do so)** We all have challenges in life, problems that are bothering us right now. It won't help your networking success rate if you become known as a whiner. That's what counsellors are for.

10. **Monopolizing the Other Person's Time:** This is a little different than what is outlined in #7 I'm so Wonderful! If you are shy or uncomfortable with networking it can be easy to stay with one person longer than you should. You are depriving both of you the opportunity to meet other people.

11. **Disrespecting a Business Card:** People tend to take their business card quite seriously. It is an extension of who they are. We aren't as serious about it as say the Japanese however, picking your teeth with someone's business card is a not a great way to make friends and influence people.

12. **Hit & Run: (Acting like a Shark)** Sharks are a type of networker who go to a business networking event with the intent of making a sale right there, right now. They don't care about you or your business. They are only interested in what they can get from you. Don't be one! And don't allow yourself to be attacked by one either!

13. **Not having Your Own Business Cards:** This portrays the image that you are not a serious networker. If you haven't even taken the time to develop and produce business cards to promote yourself, then why would I want to do business

with you? I have heard it said "Oh I don't do business cards. I take the time to write their name down on a piece of paper with their contact information. It's more personal, and then I contact them with hey remember me?" "Lame, lame, lame." That's all I can say about that comment.

14. **Eating Food While Conversing:** Many networking events offer food & beverage. Balancing a paper plate in one hand and a drink in the other can be challenging when reaching your hand out to shake another's. My personal belief is that if I am eating, I will stand to the side and chow down, then when finished I will resume networking. I have had to stand an awfully long time with a plate of food in my hand, while listening to another to avoid appearing rude. Be careful of spinach dips. Spinach stuck to your teeth can take your conversational partner's focus to different directions than what you intended.

15. **Networking While Inebriated:** You are your own liquor control board. If you can't handle your liquor without getting mouthy, don't drink! What you say and do may come back to haunt you.

～

48. THE SECRET TO BEING A POWER NETWORKER REVEALED!

O kay, if you are thinking that is a pretty bold statement to make, I would agree with you.

Any time that you see the words 'secret' and 'revealed' together in the same sentence, I would advise caution. It is usually followed by a request for payment for the content of the secret to be revealed to you. I am going to reveal the secret to you for free, after all, it was given to me at no charge.

The secret to being a power networker is... [drum roll please] ACTASIF.

Say what?

Simply put, to be a power networker i.e. one who is effective in their networking activities, **act as if** you already are successful. You may find it somewhat anticlimactic to hear this one word secret if you haven't heard the expression before. Another way of saying it would be "fake it until you make it." Or with a bit of a stretch it could be "mind over matter."

"Act as if it were impossible to fail." -- Dorothea Brande

Apparently your mind doesn't know the difference between imagining and reality. You would think it would. I'm sure if I acted upon some of my imaginings as though they were real, I could find myself in a lot of trouble. So if your mind doesn't know the difference and you have the idea that you are going to be fearful or perhaps you expect the networking event to be extremely stressful, then guess what? It will be stressful and cause you to be afraid. On the other hand if you go to the event feeling confident, perhaps with the attitude of whatever happens happens, then you might achieve different results.

Any effective sports coach is using this technique extensively. They spend a lot of their time working with the athlete in having them envision every aspect of their performance in their minds long before the actual live event.

If you are a Law of Attraction believer this is an example of a self-fulfilling prophecy, or even an example of the adage "You create your own reality."

My first experience with the **ACTASIF** philosophy was in my early years in Toastmasters. Toastmasters International is the world's leading provider of inexpensive communication & leadership skills training. As a new speaker I found it stressful to stand at the front of the room, with everybody staring at me and being acutely aware of my own nervousness. It surprised me to learn that even though I was shaking and fearful inside while delivering my presentation, it was not noticed by those watching and listening to me. There is a difference between inner & outer states. Yet, I am sure that we can all think of an example of a speaker where their outward appearance was one of terror, which would likely be a magnification of their interior state at the time.

What I learned was the power of imagery. Before my presentations I would stand at the front of the room or wherever my delivery area would be and I would envision myself being successful. In my mind I would see an audience hanging on every word I said. They were nodding in appreciation of the content I was delivering and they were laughing profusely at all of my jokes. I was a success... even before I delivered the presentation.

When it came time to deliver my presentation live, it wasn't stressful because I had already delivered the presentation in my mind and was successful. I will admit that quite often the live presentations didn't go quite as wonderful as in my imagination or some of the humour fell flat, but it didn't create any undue stress for me.

Every time you make a presentation, and survive it, which you are likely to do, you incrementally build your self-confidence. Self-confidence is somewhat like a bank account --- the more successes you have in life the more is added to your self-confidence balance.

When you undertake an endeavour that requires self-confidence, you dig into that balance and you use some of it. Unlike a bank account, using up some of your balance actually causes your balance to increase. The more risks you take and successfully overcome, the more your self-confidence will increase. Unlike a bank account though, if you don't use it, you will lose it. Maintaining a healthy self-confidence level requires practice.

I have found this very same imagery technique i.e. ACTASIF to be successful when I attend networking events. Before going to the event, perhaps while I am driving there, I envision myself having good quality conversations with the people I meet where I am not the least bit nervous. I see myself making some new connections I can both provide value to and receive value in return.

I would challenge you to test this method. When preparing to attend a networking event where you usually would experience anxiety over, try imagining yourself being successful with your networking. Envision yourself having successful and rewarding conversations. Then when you are actually at the event act as if you are successful. Don't forget, you already were successful in your mind. As Captain Jean Luc Picard from Star Trek The Next Generation would say "Make it so!"

~

"NEVER LET THE FEAR OF STRIKING OUT GET IN YOUR WAY". – BABE Ruth, 1895-1948, American Baseball Player

"The antidotes to fear and ignorance are desire and knowledge. Propel yourself forward by learning what you need to learn to do what you want to do." --- Brian Tracy

"Most people are paralyzed by fear. Overcome it and you take charge of your life and your world." --- Mark Victor Hansen

"If you do not do the thing you fear, the fear controls your life." --- Brian Tracy

49. WHY PEOPLE RESIST NETWORKING

This chapter is based upon a podcast by Dr. Ivan Misner the Founder of BNI (Business Networking International). In the podcast Dr. Misner outlines four different reasons people resist networking. This article is intended to help you identify those four reasons to see if any of them are causing you to resist networking.

Misner's research consisted of querying BNI members on Facebook and other media and was based upon a hundred or so submissions. While perhaps not scientifically accurate it offers some suggestions that make sense.

Misner questions why business owners would resist networking as a way to expand or market their business. Given the prohibitive cost of advertising you would think business networking would have a higher return on investment on a much lower expenditure.

Top Four Reasons that Business Owners Resist Networking:

1. **Not Confident:** This was the most popular reason cited. Many business owners lack the confidence to network effectively. The thought of interacting with strangers was

paralyzing. Misner identified a mixture of low-confidence, shyness and an under-estimation of what a business owner could contribute were cited as reasons not to network.

2. **Too Busy!** Many business owners feel they don't have enough time to network in their already busy day. Many people believe you have to give up something or another activity to be able to network rather than viewing it as an essential part of doing business. Taking time to network can cause stress on top of other commitments. Misner says by using 'no time' as a reason for not networking, they really don't understand what the goals of networking are.

3. **Inpatient for Results:** Networking doesn't always give immediate results. If you are in a sales position in a large firm you will likely be under pressure to make sales and produce results

4. **Networking can take time and it takes follow-up.** Many sales people become desperate and desperation is not marketable. Misner says that "Networking is not a get rich quick scheme. It is more like farming than hunting."

5. **Networking is Selling:** Many people are frightened about being sold to or they are frightened about having to pitch their product or service before a large room full of people. They don't realize networking is not live face-to-face cold calling. Some would disagree. Misner says "Networking isn't something that you do to someone, it is something that you do with them." Networking is more about listening to the other person than it is talking about yourself and getting to learn more about the other person. Comfort leads to opportunity and opportunity leads to referral.

～

"To position yourself ahead of your competition, you have to negotiate from strength: Who you are, who you are perceived to be, who is on your side." --- Patricia Fripp

50. CONSIDER JOINING A BUSINESS NETWORKING/REFERRAL GROUP

Y ou might be thinking "If I'm shy, why would I want to set myself up for a situation bound to cause me anxiety?" That's a fair question. If you believe joining one would increase your anxiety, it likely will. It is the law of a 'self-fulfilling' prophesy coming to play.

On the other hand, there is value in surrounding yourself with like-minded successful people. Business networking groups are based upon the concept of business people working together to help build each other's businesses. When used effectively it can be like having a sales force working on your behalf.

Two obstacles that come into play with shy and/or anxious networkers are you will have to step out of your comfort zone to meet new people and the possibility you might make a financial commitment you will regret making. Either of these scenarios can cause anxiety.

To set up the upcoming sections on how to **determine** if a referral/networking group is suitable for you and **how** **to make** a networking/referral group work for you I first will give a quick overview of them. There are at least two models I am aware of i.e. paid referrals or non-paid referrals.

I'll start off with the non-paid model. I believe that BNI (Business Networking International), founded by Dr. Ivan Misner was one of the first groups to formalize a model of referral networking, in a club-like setting. Since then, other groups have developed around the world that share some or all of BNI's base features.

Members get together on a regular basis, often sharing a breakfast or lunch and get to know each other better for the purpose of promoting each other's business. Many referral groups keep track of statistics as to how many referrals were generated by the group as well as revenue generated from those referrals. When referrals are made there is no exchange of funds between members, nor is a debt incurred to that particular member. Membership fees include a membership portion to offset the group's operational expenses as well as the cost of your meal, if the group meets at a restaurant for a shared meal.

As for the paid-for-referral groups they differ slightly. You will still be required to pay a membership fee but you will also pay a predetermined referral or 'finder's fee' whenever a fellow group member makes a referral that creates revenue for you.

Both of these models provide educational opportunities at their regular meetings as well as opportunities for members to deliver their elevator pitch and perhaps a longer presentation as to what their business is about and what it offers.

Now let's move on to some practical tips on how to make a non-pay for referrals group work for you. I was a member of one for about two years. One of the basic rules for the non-pay for referrals groups is they only allow one member from each occupation.

For example, there would only be one accountant, one realtor, one home building contractor. The idea is that if there are more than one of each it can make it challenging as to who you would direct your referral to. I suppose it could create a popularity contest coming into play if you had the choice of two but you liked one better. Some groups will allow more than one from each occupational field if they provide different services. A criminal lawyer, that is a lawyer that works with criminals, not a criminal themselves, would not be in competition with one that specialized in wills or real estate. (It's hard not to fit a lawyer joke in when you can.) They can likely refer business to each other. Mortgage brokers, real estate agents, property value assessors will likely be of support to each other.

Here are some helpful tips to aid you in your consideration of whether to join a particular networking/referral group. You may have several choices if you live in a larger community.

Before Joining:

Tip One – Consider Day of the week & time of day: When considering joining a non-pay for referrals group, research your options as to time of day & location. One of the secrets to being successful in your networking/referral group membership is to attend on a regular basis. Make sure the day and time you are considering is consistent with your ability to attend on a regular basis.

Tip Two - Research the group on-line: Determine if the group has a web-presence. Are they actively promoting their members on their website or are they merely marketing membership to the group?

Tip Three – Research the members: Assuming the group has an on-line presence, do they feature profiles of their members? Do you recognize or know any of the members personally? If you do, this can help make your joining and transitioning into an effective and productive referral group member a lot easier. It is always good to have a friend on the 'inside'.

If you don't know or recognize anyone, take a look at their individual profiles and their occupational fields. Are any of them similar to your business or would likely do business with the same customers you do?

Tip Four - Determine how many members are currently in the

group? A group with few members could indicate it has some leadership problems or one that has the inability to market the advantages of joining their group. It may merely mean many members left the group before you checked them out. It happens! Bigger does not necessarily mean better! The referral statistics are of greater value to you.

Tip Five - Research the venue: If you join the group you are going to be spending a lot of time there. Is the restaurant/hotel/meeting room somewhere you wouldn't be embarrassed inviting a guest to attend?

Tip Six - Attend a meeting before making your decision: You are going to invest your time and money on joining a group. Ensure you are making the right decision. Attend a meeting and get a feel for the group. Ask yourself these questions:

- Are the leaders visible and actually leading?
- Does the group actively promote the members seeking and providing referrals to each other or do they seem more like a social group?
- Do all members seem to be treated equally i.e. there are no prima donnas that get all of the attention?
- Do the members seem to be having fun being together?
- Ask some of the members if they have found being a member of this particular group has gained them referrals and subsequent revenue.

Tip Seven: Determine the group's rules. Some groups have rules or standards of conduct. An example might be having to pay your membership dues in advance, not after the fact. You may be required to send someone in your place if you are unable to attend. Some groups have fairly rigid attendance standards and should you not be able to attend as much as you are expected to, the club may choose to allow someone else in as a member to replace you and your occupational field.

Tip Eight: Determine who the leaders of the group are. I would suggest asking the President or the Chair of the group out for coffee. It gives you a good opportunity to learn more about the history of the group and how particular members might be of advantage to you in helping to grow your business.

In our next chapter we will take a look at some helpful tips to maximize your networking/referral group membership.

~

"Networking is simply the cultivating of mutually beneficial, give and take, win-win relationships. It works best, however, when emphasizing the "give' part." -- Bob Burg

51. STRATEGIES TO GET THE MOST OUT OF YOUR BUSINESS NETWORKING/REFERRAL GROUP

You have done your research and decided upon a referral group that works for you. So now what? How do you get value out of your membership?

Strategy One: Develop your 30-second to one minute elevator pitch. Most groups will allow you that much time to promote yourself. Practice saying it out loud, even to family members or the family pet if they will listen. The intent is you become comfortable saying it without getting nervous. This will go a long way in reducing the performance anxiety that often accompanies shyness.

Strategy Two: Practice saying your name out loud and the name of your business. If you haven't developed your USP (Universal Sales Proposition) now is the time to do so.

Strategy Three: For your fellow group members to be able to promote your business you need to teach them exactly what it is you do or have to offer. If the group offers a member showcase as part of the meeting i.e. where members have an allotted amount of time to present to the group, get yourself on the speaking schedule. Prepare and practice a presentation that introduces yourself to the group.

Subsequent presentations can allow you to demonstrate your expertise or knowledge on a particular subject.

Strategy Four: Obtain a membership list for your group and send a postcard or thank you note to all of the members of the group thanking them for allowing you to join them. It is a great way to plug your business and offer your services to your fellow members.

Strategy Five: Develop a plan to go out for 'coffee talk' with each of your fellow members to get to know them better and to share with them what your business is all about.

Strategy Six: If you are finding the networking in your club to be too challenging and out of your comfort zone consider asking one of your fellow members to mentor you. Some people seem to be natural networkers but in fact they are highly skilled. If they can do it, you can too!

Strategy Seven: As a member you are expected to help build the club. Invite your fellow business colleagues out to a meeting. If you are already a friend of theirs it can help leverage your reach with your fellow members.

Strategy Eight: Some groups tend to sit down at tables as soon as they arrive in the meeting room. Arrive five to ten minutes before the meeting starts and plan on staying an extra five or so at the end. It can be a great way to have a quick conversation with a member you haven't had the chance to get to know very well yet.

Strategy Nine: Try to sit across or beside someone different at each meeting. Again, a great way to get to know your fellow members in a social setting.

Strategy Ten: Befriend a guest. This can be a good way to meet a potential business connection, in a safe setting. Even if they don't join your group you can still develop a relationship with them.

Strategy Eleven: Once you are comfortable with the group consider taking on a leadership role. Serving as a 'servant leader' can help develop your influence which can help develop your reputation as the 'one to go to' for help.

Probably one of the biggest challenges members face is they don't see results as fast as they would like to. It takes time to build relationships. People like to do business with people they know and trust. Learning to trust people and becoming a person others trust may take a while.

∾

"Each of us has a spark of life inside us, and our highest endeavour ought to be to set off that spark in one another." --- Kenny Ausubel

"Success is neither magical nor mysterious. Success is the natural consequence of consistently applying basic fundamentals." Jim Rohn

"You cannot succeed by yourself. It's hard to find a rich hermit." Jim Rohn

52. FIND A NETWORKING MENTOR

One of the quickest ways to develop a skill or self-confidence in any endeavour can be to work with a mentor. Mentors are people who have "been there... done that!" as the expression goes.

Finding a networking mentor can be a little challenging perhaps. I am asking you to network with someone who you have observed to be an effective networker themselves and asking them to share with you some of the secrets or skills they have learned that work for them.

Okay, I might be asking you to step out of your comfort zone a little but that really is what it is all about. Personal growth only comes when you challenge yourself.

A mentor can come in the form of a formalized relationship or an informal one. Maybe you have a business colleague or friend that seems to be very successful in how they network. Go ahead and ask them for some tips. Most people are flattered that you ask them for some advice.

It can be as simple as asking somebody to go out for coffee.

$\sim$

"LEARN FROM THE EXPERTS. STUDY SUCCESSFUL MEN AND WOMEN AND do what they do and you'll be successful too." --- Brian Tracy

Motivational speaker Anthony Robbins once said, "If you want to be successful, find someone who achieved the results you want and copy what they do, and you'll achieve the same results."

"We could all use a little coaching. When you're playing the game, it's hard to think of everything." --- Jim Rohn

53. EVEN MORE TIPS & TECHNIQUES TO NETWORK LIKE A PRO

I s your net **working**? No, really is it?

Are you getting a good return on investment (ROI) for the amount and time and effort you are investing in your networking efforts? You are networking aren't you?

As an entrepreneur with multiple 'potential' streams of income as I call them, it is crucial that I get out there and network. For people to do business with me, at least on the local level, they first have to know me. That's where the networking comes in, face-to-face. Yes, it is necessary to get off of the computer sometimes and actually meet people. This becomes an ordeal if you are shy.

In the first part of the book **Power Networking for Shy People: Tips & Techniques for Moving from Shy to Sly!** I outlined a system I developed to help overcome my shyness, get me out networking and moving me to fame and fortune. I'm still waiting for that last part though... waiting... waiting...

I've been sharing that system with you throughout this updated version of the book.

In this section **Even More Tips & Techniques...** I focus on topics that didn't fit into the other sections of the book. Each chapter is a self-contained article on a particular facet of effective networking drawn from my series of articles entitled **Is Your Net Working?**

You may recognize some of the content from early chapters and it may be taken in a slightly different direction. Hopefully it will serve as a review rather than an annoyance.

Recent research is indicating that some 50% of North Americans describe themselves as being shy. If you are shy, you are in good company. Networking can be daunting if you are challenged with shyness, throughout this book I share practical tips & techniques I have used successfully. If they work for me they will likely work for you.

≈

54. TOO SHY TO NETWORK?

S ound familiar?

- "Do your hands start **sweating** and your legs **shake** with the thought of having to not only attend a business networking session but **actually talk to people**?"
- "Do you feel paralyzed by the fear of rejection when you are at a business networking event?
- "Would you rather have a root canal than attend a business networking event?
- "Would you rather send an e-mail to a business lead than meet them in person?"

WELL IF ANY OF THESE APPLY ... YOU MAY BE SHY!

"Get over it!" That's what our extroverted friends would say. "Just do what we do!"

Life isn't that simple. We aren't all extroverts and it would probably be a noisy world if we were. **Being shy isn't a personal defect.**

YOU AREN'T THE ONLY ONE OUT THERE, EVEN IF IT FEELS LIKE IT sometimes. The world is full of shy people and that **doesn't** prevent you from being an **effective** networker and **reaping the benefits** that networking can bring to your business.

Shyness can be defined as a reticence and self-consciousness, not just in stressful social situations but over-all.

Studies in shyness back in 1972 at Stanford University's Shyness Clinic indicated that 40% of Americans considered themselves to be shy. Nowadays, closer to 50% are likely to say they are shy. You would think that with all of the advancements in modern sciences and the humanities that we would become more outgoing. Perhaps all those advances are what are causing us to become shyer.

It has been said that it started with ATMs and Walkmans. We are no longer obligated to stand in line at our financial institutions to do our banking. We can do it with a machine. The opportunity to talk to your neighbour while standing in line is lost as well as small talk with the teller. Grocery stores and many other ones now have self-check-outs. No need to interact with a check-out clerk anymore. Walkmans allowed us to walk and listen to our music, for our ears only, a great way to escape unwanted conversations. The Walkman developed into MP3 players and smart phones that while getting smaller in size have offered us more ways to escape the real world.

The traditional family is no longer traditional. The days where the father went to work, the mother stayed home and the children went to school, all to come home at the end of the day to share a meal and their adventures of the day only exists in reruns of Leave it to Beaver. Traditional meals were replaced by TV dinners, then microwaveable ones. Fast food has become even faster and arguably not even food anymore. The opportunity to develop one's communication and conversing skills around the family dinner table may be lost forever.

I believe you can place the condition of shyness on a continuum. On one end you would have an individual who is painfully shy. The mere thought of having to go to a networking event and conversing with people could be enough to cause them to have a panic attack. Any situation where one feels that they are likely to die is to be avoided at all costs.

At the other end of continuum would be someone who experiences some mild apprehension about participating in networking events. They feel the apprehension but go ahead and do it anyways.

So how do we move towards the end of the continuum to the point where we are less apprehensive about meeting and socializing with people, even to the point of enjoying it?

As a registered nurse working most of my career in mental health I realize there will be some individuals who will only be able to move forward by taking an anti-anxiety medication such as lorazepam to reduce their anxiety. This is only recommended for those who have severe difficulty. Despite what some physicians will say, these medications are only to be used for short durations. Coming off of the medication can be as stressful for the person as the situation medication was taken for in the first place.

I believe the secret to becoming more social i.e. moving away from shy is a cognitive behavioural one combined with skill development. There are a few clinical modalities that might be of use. Some might say it is not important to know why you are shy or what causes your symptoms. "Forget about it, move forward, do it anyways!" A Reality Therapy approach might be "You are shy because you choose to be. What are you going to do to change it and become more social?"

A Solutions Focused approach would likely say something like "Tell me what it would look like if you were no longer shy. What would you be doing? Who would you be talking to? What would you be saying to them? How would you be feeling?" They wouldn't be focusing on the past, only on how the future could be.

I'm a proponent of the Solutions Focused Method combined with education and experience.

There are a lot of parallels with the fear of public speaking and shyness in social situations. Over the past 25 years I have been honing my public speaking skills by studying public speaking as a member of Toastmasters. I regularly challenge myself by delivering presentations and speeches, both within my club with fellow members and out in the public.

Darren Lacroix, the 2001 World Champion of Public Speaking describes the secret to becoming a better public speaker as being "Stage time, stage time, stage time." I believe the secret to becoming less shy and more self-confident is similar. You need to face your fear of networking by getting out there and doing it, over and over again.

Within the Toastmasters program we develop our skills by continually moving forward in our educational program and raising the bar as they say in increasing the challenges we face. The more we speak in public, the more we desensitize ourselves and reduce the power anxiety has over us. The Toastmaster's program also offers constructive feedback as a way to maximize our self-development.

An overall plan to reduce shyness and increase self-confidence would be wise to include joining Toastmasters. Membership will provide you ample opportunities to both develop your communication and leadership skills but also plenty of opportunities to network in social situations.

Research the topic of business networking. You will find that while there is lots written about the subject, finding practical tips and techniques can be challenging to find.

Look for networking events in your community. Don't expect to be a power networker from the beginning. As they say you can't expect to run before you can walk. Learn what you can about the organization facilitating the event. What type of people attend the events? Is it purely social in nature or are people expecting to network for business opportunities?

If you are shy and it is important you network, accompany a friend to the next business networking event, preferably someone who is a little more outgoing than you are. Ask them to introduce you to some people they know who may be of benefit for you to meet.

As I said in the introduction, if almost 50% of people are saying that they are shy, then odds are there will be a high number of shy people at any event. You won't be alone!

～

"THE REASON FOR LIVING IS TO HAVE GREAT RELATIONSHIPS, TO HAVE people you love and respect, and who love you and respect you." --- Brian Tracy

"Don't judge each day by the harvest you reap, but by the seeds you plant." --- Robert Louis Stevenson

55. SO WHAT'S YOUR STORY?

"Nice day eh?"

"Too bad about the Canucks!"

"Isn't this weather something?"

We have heard them all before... meaningless comments that are more likely to end a conversation than to advance it.

For the many people we encounter during our daily travels perhaps this is all that is needed. If we had long drawn out conversations with everyone, we likely wouldn't accomplish everything we need to in a day.

However, attending and getting the most out of a business networking session is another story [pun intended]. This is the perfect opportunity for you to share your success stories. A success story is a short, punchy anecdote. It teaches your conversation partner about your business, what you are interested in and hopefully gives the listener a reason to get to know you better.

All that in about 2 to 3 minutes!

This concept was reinforced to me recently when I attended a local Chamber of Commerce event. A fellow networker asked me how my society was going. I was the Chairman for a local entrepreneur society at the time. I went into my spiel of the challenges we were facing in moving forward. One step forward, two steps backwards. I realized later I had missed a perfect opportunity to promote the volunteer opportunities available within the society as well as the opportunity to share my vision for the future of the society. I had invested a lot of time and energy in moving the society forward and I should have been prepared to share the story with whoever was willing to hear it.

It is often said that misery loves company. Does your present conversational companion really want to share your misery? I have met far too many people over the years whose default mode is what I call 'poor pitiful me.' I recognize it readily having used it myself in my early years. Many people find it easier to share with others how awful life is treating them rather than sharing success stories. The logical conclusion would be that if you were coming from a position of self-pity then you are unlikely to have a collection of success stories.

Many of our mothers have taught us not to talk about ourselves. "Nobody likes braggers!" Walt Whitman is quoted as saying "If you done it, it ain't bragging." While not grammatically correct, it is the essence of sharing your story.

Each of us has multiple personas based on the different roles we have in life. Some describe it 'as wearing many hats.' We may be at a business networking session to market our business but we still have our different personas with us at all times and we should be prepared to share a success story related to any of those personas if the opportunity arises.

As in many endeavours, the key to success is advance preparation. Take stock of what is new and exciting in your life that others would appreciate hearing about. Share your enthusiasm!

So how does one create a good story? You would think the answer would be to start at the beginning but you would be wrong. I would suggest you start creating your story by developing the ending first.

What do you hope to achieve by sharing a story? Are you hoping someone will follow you in your cause? Will you be educating somebody on a topic or issue that is of importance to you or is your intention merely to entertain? The most important part to remember with developing your conclusion to your story is "What do you want the listener to take away from your story?"

With your 'take away' clearly in your mind you can now carry on to developing the opening for your story. This is the part where you want to grab your listener's attention so they are eager to listen to the rest of the story.

Using fishing with a rod as an analogy, your story's opening is the bait you are using to attract the fish to bite. The content of your story being the moving the rod up and down praying for a bite. Setting the hook and landing the fish being the conclusion of your story.

I left out the part about drinking a lot of beer as I recall from my long ago days of fishing. Your story's opening should be short and to the point, yet be teasing enough for the listener to want to hear more.

A: "So what's new?"

B: "Not much, same ole, same ole. How about you?"

A: "The same. Business sucks. Can't make a decent living in this economy."

B: "We'll catch you later on the flip side."

A: "Okay, see ya."

Does this sound familiar? 'A' set up the discussion with "So what's new?" 'B' missed the opportunity to share a story about what is new and exciting in their life. Neither gained anything from this interaction.

You are at a business networking event and you are asked the very same question "So what's new?" Now what do you do? It's story time! If you have had previous conversations with this individual on a particular subject I would suggest updating them on anything new with the same subject.

If you haven't had previous conversation with your fellow networker, the field is wide open. You can talk about what's new and exciting about your business. Often there is an awkward period of time just after two networkers have introduced themselves to each other and delivered their elevator pitches. If they haven't found common areas of interest there can be a lull while each rapidly thinks of where to take the conversation. Instead of waiting for the "What's new" question, you could interject into the conversation and take it in a different direction. Yours!

So what's new? Go ahead ... ask me!

"I've been working as a registered nurse for over 40 years and having worked with thousands of people over the years I thought I had seen everything. The other day I..."

"As a master organizer I help organizations create events that raise attention for their cause as well as much needed funds. One of my clients was pleasantly surprised when I..."

"One of the things in life I am passionate about is in honing my communication and leadership skills. I've been a member of Toastmasters for over 25 years and continue to learn something new. The other day I learned..."

"I've been doing a lot of writing lately. One project is a series of articles related to business networking entitled "Is Your Net Working." My latest one is about..."

So ... what's your story?

～

"You have to have confidence in your ability, and then be tough enough to follow through." --- Rosalynn Carter

"The most important single ingredient in the formula of success is knowing how to get along with people." --- Theodore Roosevelt

56. CLOSE ENCOUNTERS OF THE NETWORKING KIND

H ave you ever wondered how close to stand to another person when conversing in a 1 to 1 at a business networking session? Okay, maybe I do have too much spare time as they say but I am sure this is a question many people have asked.

While I don't have a definitive answer, I do have some thoughts on the matter. Many factors including gender, culture, trust, past experiences and self-confidence come into play.

Looking at it from a self-defence, self-preservation perspective, it is helpful to think of each of us having an invisible circle or a safety zone around us. As a preservation measure we tend to keep strangers outside of our safety zone and only let people we trust or are comfortable with into our comfort zone.

In North America our personal safety zone tends to be about three feet in diameter around us. The same distance as our outstretched arm and fist or our outstretched leg if we were intending to strike or kick someone in self-defence. Our comfort zone i.e. the area where we will let those that we trust into tends to be about 18 to 30 inches in diameter.

In a business networking session I'm sure we don't attend with the idea we are going to have to physically defend ourselves. I believe this is a situation that can cause stress in some people in networking situations. To have an effective discussion with someone who you are meeting for the first time as in a business networking session often means you are permitting a stranger to enter your comfort zone. Crowded, noisy rooms tend to necessitate drawing in closer to the other person just to be able to hear them well.

While it is socially acceptable for women to hold or touch each other while in conversation, even in a first meeting encounter, the same cannot be said about two men conversing.

You may not even be aware you have a comfort zone until someone invades it. That feeling of anxiousness, uneasiness may be your subconscious calling to your attention something isn't right. Perhaps this is the time to take a step backwards to continue your conversation.

If you are confident in your networking conversations, allowing others into your comfort zone and paying close attention to the conversation by actively participating in it can go a long way in building your reputation as an effective networker and somebody worth meeting and getting to know.

Many networkers have challenges of inserting themselves into groups that have already formed and are actively discussing a topic. A group where the members are standing close enough to converse with each other, yet not within each other's comfort zones, would likely be a group that would be open to having someone else join them.

On the other hand, two people standing very close together, perhaps a little ways away from the rest of the group would seem to be having an intimate conversation and would not likely be open to someone joining them. If they were to separate from each other that could indicate that the private or intimate stage of their conversation has concluded and they were now open to be joined by others.

You can learn a lot by observing others. In your next networking session observe how people are standing. Are they close together or far apart? Does an individual networker use the same technique with everyone they meet or do they vary their closeness in conversation? Try out some different distances to your conversational partner and see how it feels to you.

∾

"NETWORK CONTINUALLY -- 85 PERCENT OF ALL JOBS ARE FILLED through contacts and personal references." --- Brian Tracy

"Business success comes from identifying and targeting specific customer groups or market segments for your product or service." --- Brian Tracy

57. NAME DROPPING FOR FUN & PROFIT

Does this sound familiar? You are at a business networking session and you are captivated by a speaker who wants to regale you with a litany of important people they have supposedly recently spent time with. "Oh, the other day I had coffee with the Mayor..." "I was just saying the very same thing to my good friend XXX, you know he owns half the town." "Yeah, my best friend is the Crown Attorney and she was telling me..."

To coin a phrase... "blah, blah, blah, yaddey, yaddey, yaddey!"

I suppose it is a fact of life we need to accept. There are some people in life who need to name drop to build up their ego or their sense of importance. On the other hand, I have met some people who are so narcissistic it would never occur to them their listener doesn't know the individuals who have been offered as proof of something, nor would even care if they did know them.

Having worked in mental health/psychiatry for 40+ years I have learned at least one concept that has served me well and it is 'all behaviour has meaning.' The challenge is we don't often know what the meaning is or what purpose it is serving and likely the other individual doesn't either.

A person who has a tendency to drop names of important people into conversation, and the term 'important' is subjective, could be nervous or lack self-confidence in a 1-1 conversation. Talking about 'important' people could be a maladaptive coping mechanism, one to relieve the individual's anxiety. If the person they are talking about is well known or popular the concept seems to be that some of that popularity will rub off on them. It is probably similar to bragging about one's self.

Once you recognize the individual is monopolizing the conversation and playing a game of "look who I know!" what do you do about it?

Not taking action is one choice. You could continue to listen to the one-sided conversation. Odds are if they have dropped some names into conversation they likely have quite a few more to offer. It would probably be a good idea to extricate yourself by excusing yourself before you doze off.

Another option could be to derail the conversation i.e. take it off its likely track by saying something to the effect of "Oh you know XXX. I have been wanting to meet them for a while. Could you introduce us or arrange a meeting?"

This action on your part could have a positive outcome if the individual actually does know the V.I.P. and can introduce you to them. Or if they don't really know them, they may start to back paddle i.e. change the topic or avoid the request made of them and keep the conversation going in a direction where they continue to own it.

A third option could be a variation of the old "See you later alligator!" At a business networking function odds are high you can leave this one-sided conversation and move on to a more productive one.

Is there a time when it is appropriate for you to name drop? Yes, I believe so. Name dropping or inserting another person's name into the conversation can help build your credibility as someone who is well-connected, one who has a good understanding on a particular topic and it can even develop your personal influence.

Some examples might be:

- When having a conversation about a particular topic, issue or problem and you know someone who has faced a similar situation, you could mention their name and describe the lessons they learned as they dealt with the subject.
- You could offer your services as an intermediary and propose to introduce the person you are speaking with to someone who you know that could be in a position to assist them.
- At a later date, perhaps at a "getting to know you" coffee meeting you could explore with each other who each of you knows and if there is a possibility any of these connections could be of value in helping with a current need.

I hope through this article I have been able to raise your awareness to the "name-dropper" style of networker and offer you some ideas on how to deal with them. But then again... name dropping can be an effective networking tool if used effectively. Try it out and see how it works for you. Even better still... become one of those people other people fit into their conversations.

~

"IF YOU DON'T THINK YOU CAN DO IT, WHO WILL? YOU CONTROL THE most important tool in success, your mind." --- Jeffrey Gitomer

58. FINDING COMMON INTERESTS

Meeting somebody for the first time as in a networking situation can often leave you stuck for words. Your counterpart delivers their elevator pitch and then as they pause to catch their breath they utter "so what do you do?" You go on to deliver your well-rehearsed pitch for your business. But did the two of you really communicate?

Communication is a two-way process. While the other person is sharing their story, you need to be listening closely to them. This isn't the time to be practicing your own story in your head. This is the time to listen. Imagine that there will be a test after your partner delivers their personal story. Besides trying to figure out what their business is about, you should be listening for statements or beliefs that are similar to yours. Perhaps you have had similar experiences as they have described.

Research has shown people like to do business with people similar to themselves. It is also often said people will do business with friends before strangers. So how do you rapidly turn an impromptu exchange of elevator pitches into a 'best buddies' scenario?

Well, sometimes it does happen by accident. You will meet somebody and very rapidly find you hit it off as the saying goes. If you are a Law of Attraction follower, you would say you are resonating. You are on the same wave length. But more often than naught it doesn't go that way and can be awkward at best.

The solution lays in you taking charge of the conversation. By charge, I don't mean to take control and dominate it at the other's expense. I mean to be proactive and direct the conversation in the way you want it to go. Research has also shown people respond well when you ask them questions about something they have just said, asking them to expand upon a point perhaps. The usual questions of who, how, why, when and where can be used to elicit further info effectively as long as you don't come across as giving them the third degree. "Where were you on the night of...? Can anybody vouch for your where-abouts" may not be the way to win friends and influence people.

Asking more questions of the person is also a highly recommended traditional sales communication method i.e. you use the information you have just gathered to tailor your sales pitch for the individual. While it may be okay if you are actually in a sales situation I wouldn't recommend it in first-contact networking encounter. As I said most people will respond well to probing questions as long as they feel you are eager to learn more from them. You will know fairly quickly if you are dealing with a paranoid individual. They are out there.

Once you determine whether you have common interests, don't forget to talk about the possibility of doing business together or helping each other with referrals. Who knows, you may start off business networking and end up with a new best friend.

It can be a great feeling when coming home from a networking event and looking at the stack of business cards you have collected. You even spoke at length to many of the card-donators. Some, it can be a little difficult to recall who they actually were. "Now was he the tall fellow with the bad hair piece.... or was he?" You've probably experienced that scenario more than once. And you know what... perhaps some of the business people you gave your precious business card to are thinking something similar. Hopefully not about your bad hair though.

For effective business networking I recommend the *quality* over *quantity* method of networking. Some would say networking is a numbers game, the more you meet the higher the chances of meeting someone who can benefit you. Take for example you are meeting someone for the first time and if the setting and conditions permit, they deliver their elevator pitch and you return with yours. Then comes the awkward moment, what to say next. You can either carry on conversing about something of no consequence "Nice day, eh?" until one of you tires or you can explore common interests.

Assuming you have a common interest I would suggest you take the lead in the conversation in getting the other to expand upon the commonality or something they had previously said.

Many networkers make the mistake of trying to sell their product or themselves at this juncture. Your goal should be to arrange to meet them at another time, perhaps for coffee, to discuss those common areas further. Even though many of us are electronically connected to our offices by our smart phones and can likely check to see if we are available at a certain date and time to make a coffee date, we likely won't. When you suggest meeting for coffee, later, if the person is willing to set up a date and time, on the spot, I would go with it. Location can always be determined later by e-mail.

If they aren't willing to set a time and date, I would refer to their business card and say something to the effect of "Can I reach you at this e-mail? I'll contact you next week and see if we can set up a time to get together for a quick coffee."

Unfortunately, for many networkers, this is as far as they go. They don't do the follow-up. Life gets busy, there is always one more thing to do with your business and before you know it you have lost the window of opportunity. There is a strong possibility the individual you were networking with also has a list of people they are following up with and other commitments. It is far too easy to get left by the wayside if you don't take action to stand out from the others.

The coffee get-together is the opportunity for each of you to share your business details and determine if there is enough reason to continue at another time to develop your relationship further and ideally to do business together.

You might ask "I've contacted them three times by e-mail and even left a couple voice mails but they haven't gotten back to me. What do I do next?" There could be a legitimate reason for them not getting back to you. Life happens! But they could be acting non-assertively and are actively avoiding you. I would have to respond with "If that was true, is that someone that you really want to network with or to do business with?" If you are to continue it could easily label you as a stalker.

One suggestion may be to add them to your tickler file. A couple weeks down the road, ignoring the fact they haven't acknowledged you yet, you would be justified in sending them a message something like "I just noticed we didn't get together a few weeks ago like we said we would. Where did the time go? It seems to be picking up speed. Last time we met we were discussing our common interests of... Are you still interested in getting together?" If you still don't receive a response, I would put them in the "inactive" file.

When it comes to networking, to stand out from your competition, remember to follow-up.

~

"ALL ADVANCEMENT, ALL SUCCESS AND ALL ACHIEVEMENT STARTS WITH **personal relationships and creativity.**"- -- Mark Victor Hansen

"Every farmer knows that you can't sow and reap on the same day. There is a timetable for your harvest that requires both working and waiting. Patience is a small price to pay for what you will receive." -- Neil Eskelin

"Learn to help people with more than just their jobs; help them with their lives." Jim Rohn

59. SERENDIPITY ISN'T A PLAN!

I've often heard it said in reference to 'self-help' books... "If you get only one gem or a useful tip from a book it makes all of your reading time worthwhile." While that may be true, it can have you spending a lot of time with your nose in a book.

The same principal can be applied... inefficiently... to your networking activities... "One contact can make a world of difference in your business..." In essence you are leaving your success to serendipity.

Serendipity, or leaving everything to chance, while awe-inspiring when it works, is not something you can control or count on.

Does the following scenario sound familiar? You attend a large event touted as the best networking event in town. You meet a dozen or so "new" people, new to you that is, not new to everyone else, or so it would seem. You deliver your 30-second or longer elevator pitch over the ever-increasing din in the packed room. You go home with a handful of business cards. The next day or so you face the challenge of contacting all of your warm leads. If this is an activity that you aren't fond of, that 200-pound phone handset can be quite daunting. "Hi, this is Rae. We met the other night at ..."

"Who?"

Okay, perhaps I am injecting my own inadequacies into this article but I really have heard people agree.

Here is a power networking technique to maximize your effectiveness. If your main purpose in attending a networking event is to get a handful of business cards, then go for it! An alternative option would be to meet a business colleague or friend you are comfortable with, in a setting that is conducive to conducting business and compare personal networks. "I'll show you mine... if you show me your's", so to speak. For those that are old enough to recall trading baseball or hockey player cards, this isn't what I am suggesting.

A planned approach is best. For example, I am looking for a book-keeper/accountant to take on a volunteer role in a society I lead. I would meet with somebody I know has a background in finances and I could specifically ask them who they would know in their network that might meet my search parameters. At this preliminary stage it is a matter of brainstorming contact's names. Write them down on a piece of paper. This isn't the time to be evaluating each name as to whether they might be interested in participating, your only task at this point is to generate a list of names.

The idea is to leverage your colleague's network. With social media being so prevalent nowadays, many of us are well connected. Well-connected doesn't mean we actually know or have even met the contact though. More of an e-contact if you will. It probably wouldn't be much of a surprise to find that you already know some of the names generated and they are part of your network.

Our next step is to rate each of the names we have generated as to how well your colleague knows the individual. Would the individual be surprised if you contacted them saying they were referred by your colleague? Or would your contacting the individual trigger a "Who?" response.

Generating a list of names isn't of much use unless you get their accompanying contact info. Now is the time to leverage your connections and make that net work. Make those phone calls.

PS: Don't forget to spend some time helping your colleague with their networking measures. While it can be said "It's not who you know... it's who knows you!", perhaps we need to amend it to "It's not who you know, it's who knows you know who you know!" I'll leave that for another article.

~

60. I WOULD LIKE TO INTRODUCE
...

A common anxiety-producing situation in a shy networker is when a third or more persons join the conversation and it falls upon them to introduce everyone.

Who do you introduce first? Do you use first and last names? Are you required to provide collateral information about each of the people that you introduce?

Life is getting a lot more casual these days, at least in North America but I am sure my etiquette expert friends would agree there is basic protocol that should be followed when making introductions.

Shaking hands upon meeting: Shaking hands upon meeting someone for the first time has become commonplace and is to be expected. Even if the other person is well known to you it is quite acceptable to shake hands in greeting if you haven't seen them for a while. Gender and age used to determine who reached out first but it has gone by the wayside. If you are sitting when introduced to someone for the first time it is appropriate to stand first unless you are in a restaurant or another setting that would make it difficult to do so.

Introducing peers to each other: As they are on the same social level it really doesn't matter who you introduce first. Use both their first and last names when introducing them unless you don't know the last name. "John Smith this is Jane Walker. Jane works in our marketing division. And if I'm not mistaken John you used to work in marketing didn't you?" Pronounce the names clearly so that it is easily understood and if you can provide a little collateral information about each of them do so. If you are aware of some common areas that the two individuals share it can be a great way to seed a conversation i.e. get it going.

Introducing a Superior to a Subordinate: I have some personal difficulties with the term superior if it means that they are better than me, my personal baggage. On the other hand, if it refers to the fact that they are higher up on the organizational chart than I am or perhaps more prominent in government, I can accept that.

Rule of thumb is you say the name of the superior first. "Mr. Smith I would like you to meet James Jones. He works in our Refreshments Division." The same idea applies where you would supply some additional information to seed a future conversation or to help create a point of reference to the one that is receiving the introduction.

Introducing a customer to people in your business: The old adage of "the customer always comes first" holds true in this situation. It is a good way to respect your customer. As in other introductions it is helpful to provide some collateral information about the customer or even your fellow business member you are introducing. It can also be a good time to do a quick testimonial about some aspect of your business dealings with your customer.

Introducing Women: The old way of doing so was to introduce a man to a woman. "Mary I would like you to meet John." You won't create an international incident if you were to do so but nowadays the trend seems to be to use rank as your rule. If you don't know who holds the so-called superiority, I would revert back to the old rule of man to woman. If anybody questions you, you could always say you didn't get the memo about the changes.

Introducing Older People: The old rule was to introduce the younger person to the older one, saying the name of the older person first. Now it is not so important.

❧

61. BE THE RED CAR

At a recent networking event I made comment to a woman that since having met her within the past year I was starting to see her at a lot of different events. She replied "Yeah me to. You are the red car!"

I immediately recognized the red car reference from the Law of Attraction. The idea being if you were to buy a red car or even were thinking about buying one, then you would start noticing red cars everywhere. The Universe recreates itself for you. Up until now red cars were not in your range of focus.

Now when it comes to business networking it would be advantageous for you to become that red car i.e. someone that others recognize easily.

One way to become more visible would be to attend local events that provide networking opportunities and working the room so you 'touch' many people i.e. interact with them. If you attend an event regularly, people will get used to seeing you there. It could get to the point that if you aren't in attendance someone might say "I wonder where... is?"

Power Networking For Shy People

If you are not overly comfortable with interacting in a face-to-face situation, cyberspace can be a good resource for you. Social media venues such as Twitter, Facebook & Linkedin offer plenty of opportunities to create an on-line persona. By joining locally based on-line groups you can easily interact with business people you might not meet at a networking event or in the normal course of operating your business. Both Linkedin and Facebook allow you to post updates which can help to keep your name front and center. So when you actually do meet them in person you already have something in common to talk about.

I am very active on-line promoting my articles such as this one as well as my business and events I am organizing. I also have quite a few websites that I have created and maintain. This tends to provide lots of entries in Google. If for whatever reason somebody was researching me, they would have lots of info to sift through. This works as a promotional tool for me.

I was at a Chamber of Commerce event and a young woman came up to me and said "I just had to meet you. You are everywhere!" She was referring to my presence on local social media venues. To her I had become the 'red car.' She was actively visiting the sites and my name and photo were popping up everywhere.

I believe there is an accompanying assumption. If you are seen everywhere i.e. being the red car, you are obviously well-connected, you have something of value to share and it would be worthwhile getting to know you.

How do you become the red car? It could be blue or any other colour if you don't care for red. If I had my way it would be a bright school bus yellow pickup truck. But since I don't own one and its on my wish list, perhaps seeing someone else driving one might not be so appreciated. I am a little leery about putting my thoughts about a new pickup truck out to the universe. The last time I did I had a new truck within a week. All I had to do was hit some black ice, do a 360 degree turnaround, land in a ditch, have the wheels fall off and have the truck written off.

So if you do become someone's 'red truck' use your power wisely!

~

62. BECOME A THOUGHT LEADER

W ikipedia defines a **thought leader** as being an individual or firm that is recognized as an authority in a specialized field and whose expertise is sought and often rewarded.

Would being recognized as a leader in your field or in your business make a difference to your bottom line? Is it possible for mere mortals, average people like you and I to become thought leaders?

I believe it is not only possible to become a leader in your specific field but it is in the reach of most of us to do so. With my keen interest in developing my business networking skills I am working towards becoming one of those thought leaders. I write about practical networking skills development for shy people as well as those who have some networking skills and want to improve their success rate.

Am I an expert at networking? In theory yes, in practice, not as much. I write about the subject of networking and shyness because they have caused me problems throughout my life. I've tested the tips & techniques I offer and I know from first hand experience they work. I also know the lessons I have learned can be very beneficial to others experiencing similar difficulties. Recent studies have indicated that over 50% of Americans consider themselves to be shy. That is a huge market awaiting me to become an expert.

My researching the topic of networking has been educational for me in several ways. I have learned I know more than a lot of people on the subject yet not as much as I could. My anxiety in networking situations has been steadily reducing as I become more educated on the subject and my effectiveness is increasing.

My goal is to become a thought leader on the subject of business networking. I am open to the fame and fortune that will come my way when I do so. It would be nice though if this happened a little sooner rather than later.

Is it really possible to become the thought leader on the subject you are experienced with? Perhaps it might be helpful to replace the word 'the' in the previous sentence with 'a.'

You don't have to be the top expert on your subject. You can become one of many and still be an effective thought leader. You also don't have to compete on the world stage. Odds are your local community and its surrounding geography could support you being its top thought leader on a specific subject.

So how does one become a thought leader? I will offer a few suggestions you might want to consider.

To be a thought leader you actually have to give some thought to the subject you want to be an expert in. That sounds rather obvious at first but I don't believe it is. Many entrepreneurs and business people are caught up in working in their business rather than working on their business. Day to day they provide a service or a product in their business without taking the time to think about how to grow their business so they can realize even greater revenue. Becoming a thought leader involves investing in yourself.

I believe it was Brian Tracy who said if you read about a specific subject for one hour a day, in five years you will become a world leading expert on your subject. In essence, he is referring to becoming a thought leader. Thought leaders are well read.

Thought leaders are also well spoken. Many people believe you are born with good public speaking skills or that it is a gift. There is no truth to that belief. Public speaking skills are no different than any other skills. You get better with practice and feedback providing corrective action. If you don't, you won't. It is also a matter of using it or losing it.

To continually develop your public speaking skills you need to consistently work at it. I have been working on honing my communication skills over the past 25 years as a member of Toastmasters International, the world's leading inexpensive provider of communication and leadership skills development. Whether you are an experienced speaker looking for opportunities to speak or a beginning speaker wanting to get over your stage fright, Toastmasters is the place to do so.

Speak well, speak often!

Thought leaders are good writers. The old saying that 'the pen is mightier than the sword' readily comes to mind. To be able to influence people and in turn lead them you need to be able to write in a manner that not only grabs the reader's attention, it spurs them into taking action. The challenge is in writing so your message is understood by the reader. The average North American reads at a grade seven level. Your challenge is to write so they can understand it yet not have your material so dumbed down that you insult those with higher literacy skills.

On-line bulletin boards, chat rooms and social media venues such as Linkedin have helped level the playing field for those that tend to be on the shy side. You can be as bold as you want to be with your on-line persona.

Linkedin has a relatively new feature where you can follow Thought Leaders from around the world. Some of them like Sir Richard

Branson have a couple million followers. I don't follow him but I guess a lot of people are interested in what he has to say. Others on the list have a mere 30,000 followers. Wouldn't that be nice? It helps to look at that 30,000 or so as being a number that could be achievable, assuming of course that it is something that you desired.

I'm guessing but I believe Linkedin likely has a group dedicated to almost any subject you can think of. You are allowed to follow and be a member of up to 50 groups at a time. To help gain exposure for yourself you can post questions or submit an article of interest to share with others. You can also provide answers or commentary on questions or discussions others have posted.

This can be a great way to create credibility for yourself and develop a reputation as being one who gives thought to a particular subject. It is also okay to disagree with what is written as long as you follow the rule of thumb of disagreeing with the opinion of the person rather than the person. There are ways to soften a response that differs from the writer such as "My experience has been a little different..."

To be a thought leader, or a leader of any type, you need to have followers. I am fond of a saying that goes "If you think you are leading and you turn around and see that no one is following you, then you are really just out for a walk." I think we all need to turn around every so often and see if anyone is following us.

We haven't answered the question yet of why we would even want to become a thought leader? Fame and fortune certainly would be nice but on a smaller scale there is great value in becoming the 'go to' person if a problem arises that you have the expertise to resolve.

I have been lead to believe the media is always looking for experts on a specific subject. It would be great to be on a short list of experts the media reaches out to when they need a quote or sound byte on a topical subject. This is not only great attention for you but it also raises attention for your business. It can be a great conversation starter. Can you imagine being able to respond to the question of "so... what's new?" with "Oh, I was on the Oprah show last week." We might have to settle with an interview by the local AM radio station but you never know who is listening or what it might lead to.

Followers need leaders. If you lead, people will likely follow you. This can be an effective way to develop your business network. Get to know your followers. Connect with them. Try it and see what happens. Let me know how your net's working.

∾

63. FOR A GOOD TIME CALL

I am sure most of us have heard of the practice of reading a message scrawled on a public restroom wall of "For a good time call..."

There is a usually a phone number accompanying the message. In all likelihood the individual mentioned is not aware of the advertising being done on their behalf nor would they likely agree with it. More than likely it was scrawled by an adolescent male, driven by testosterone and thinking it was pretty funny.

Having not spent any time in the women's restroom I can only assume that this practice only happens in the men's.

If the individual named actually wrote the message in question well I guess it could be attributed to some savvy targeted marketing.

Now I am not suggesting that you add this to your networking skills repertoire. In my example the call for action is "**for a good time call**..." Each of us has something to offer, whether it be a skill or our expertise. When we are networking for business we need to get the message out there as to what we do and what we have to offer.

Now, using a plumber as an example, what if we changed the

message to something like "For No More Leaky Pipes call..." A financial planner might say "We are your financial health experts. Will your money live as long as you do?" An entertainer could get away with "for a good time call..."

This in essence is your USP, which is often defined as Universal Sale Pitch or Unique Selling Proposition. Your USP is a short statement that summarizes who you are, what you do, why you are passionate about it and how you are different or better than anyone else who does it. All this in a short sentence. Yes it is definitely challenging. You may not want to do it but your competition likely is.

A memorable USP has a way of connecting you, your business and what you have to offer in a person's mind. You want your potential customer to automatically think of you when they have a problem to solve and you are likely the solution to it. The only way it will happen is you need to get in the habit of using your USP regularly, perhaps as part of your elevator pitch. You have to become known by your USP.

At the risk of self-promoting, after all I am an entrepreneur, I would offer one of my USPs. "Hi, I'm Rae Stonehouse also known as Mr. Emcee. I am an Okanagan-based full service master of ceremonies and event planner. From start to finish... we do it all!"

Or... for a good time call Rae... just not too early in the morning, too late in the evening, on weekends or in the afternoon as it cuts into my nap. But other than that...

~

64. "I PROPOSE ..." MAKING A PROPOSAL TO A BOARD OF DIRECTORS

B eing asked to sit as a Director on a Board of Directors of a nonprofit organization can be an effective way to both give back to society and a power networking technique to raise your visibility in your community. Unfortunately, most boards don't provide you with a 'User's Manual' on how to navigate the many tasks an active board takes on.

Board meetings, committee meetings, member meetings... coffee meetings, yes you will be required to participate in meetings. Lots of them! It is how things get done. Or some would have you believe.

Sometimes discussion about an agenda item can be jump started by using a proposal. An effective proposal presented both verbally and in writing, gives every member as complete a picture of the issue as possible.

Some elements to include in the verbal proposal:

- An overview which describes why this item is important and worth group time
- Goals you want the issue to achieve

- A description which details what the item is about and its history
- A list of pro's and con's

The **INTRODUCTION** presents and summarizes the problem you intend to solve and your solution to that problem, including the benefits the reader/group will receive from the solution and the cost of your solution.

The **BODY** of the proposal should explain the complete details of the solution: how the job will be done, broken into separate tasks; what method will be used to do it, including the equipment, material, and personnel that would be required; when the work will begin; and, when the job will be completed. It should also present a detailed cost breakdown for the entire job.

The **CONCLUSION** should emphasize the benefits the reader will realize from your solution to the problem and should urge the reader to action. It should be encouraging, confident and assertive in tone.

Once a proposal is introduced (and ideally it should be handed out well before the meeting so people have enough time to think about it), a listing of issues and concerns can be brain-stormed and worked through, discussion can happen about the issues and concerns, and a new, modified proposal can be drafted. Once sufficient discussion has occurred you may want to generate several alternative proposals and see if any of them work for the group. Often, by combining elements of multiple proposals, the end result is found.

Sometimes starting a discussion with a proposal can lead the group astray by starting at a particular place which may exclude other ideas or options. It can be helpful to introduce a starting proposal as just a starting place to get discussion going on the issue, rather than finished thinking about the issue.

As discussion on a subject is winding down, concerns have been aired and discussed, call for a proposal. It may be useful to have a break after the discussion to let people mingle more, then after the break call for proposals for consideration.

If you have the skills, expertise and an interest in a particular cause why not get involved with the group? Taking on a leadership role is a great way to leverage your visibility in your community and in turn increase your network. Who knows... it may even lead to a career change.

~

65. JOHNNY APPLESEED KNEW WHAT HE WAS DOING

L egend has it that Johnny Appleseed traveled the American countryside spreading apple seeds randomly, everywhere he went.

In fact, according to Wikipedia, he planted nurseries rather than orchards, built fences around them to protect them from livestock, left the nurseries in the care of a neighbour who sold trees on shares, and returned every year or two to tend the nursery.

Many people's business networking activities can be a lot like randomly spreading those apple seeds. Some might grow but most likely left to their own, they will fail to develop and eventually die off.

Relationships need to be nurtured. Often the word cultivated is used to describe what needs to take place for a relationship to grow. Both words are really describing an active interest, desire and taking action oriented steps to develop a relationship with another individual.

So how does one cultivate a relationship? I have some cynical colleagues who would say that would treat them the same way as you would cultivate mushrooms. You keep them in the dark and feed them BS [male cow manure.] I would suspect that they have few quality connections. I certainly wouldn't want to be connected to them with that attitude.

Let's leave the agriculture analogy for a while and go to back to the question of how does one cultivate a relationship?

CONSIDER THESE FOLLOWING STEPS OR ACTIONS: (THEY AREN'T necessarily in the order you would take. Relationship building can be more of a circuitous journey rather than a lineal one.)

- Research the individual. Check them out on Linkedin. Find out what their vocation and background is.
- Invite them out for coffee. Look for common interests.
- Be on the lookout for resource materials related to their interests and forward it on to them.
- Send them thank you notes or appropriate gifts to recognize help they have provided to you.
- Send congratulatory messages e.g. cards/notes by snail mail or perhaps by e-mail for important milestones both personal and business. Seeing their name in the paper can be a great opportunity to drop them a note and congratulate them, assuming it wasn't in Crime Stoppers or the Most Wanted List of course.
- If you are comfortable in doing so, send them business referrals. The Law of Reciprocity says if you do something good for somebody else they in turn will do something good for you.
- Perhaps you have heard of the concept of "unconditional love?" To successfully cultivate a relationship you can't put terms in place. Doing so could jeopardize the relationship.
- Don't appear to be a stalker with your focused interest.

So far we have been looking at <u>active</u> steps that you can take. For a relationship to develop you have to be open to sharing yourself. It can't be a one way transaction. There has to be a payoff for you as well.

Getting back to my agricultural analogy of cultivating, sometimes you have to do some pruning to help strengthen your plantings. The same thing applies to your network. There will always be people who are suspicious of your motives or intentions. Perhaps this isn't somebody you want in your network.

There will also be people who once you get to know them, you find you really don't want to associate with them. It might be necessary to sever all ties with the individual. If you aren't comfortable dealing with or relating to an individual you are unlikely to want to refer them to another connection. Their behaviour could have the undesirable affect of reflecting on you and your business.

An interesting side note mentioned in the Wikipedia article stated that apple trees grown from seed are rarely sweet or tasty, more on the sour side, which was apparently perfect for producing hard cider and applejack back in those days.

Modern day orchardists plant strains of trees that consistently produce a fruit that is desirable and marketable. There is no use in providing all the labour in cultivating a crop if you aren't able to realize a bountiful harvest.

So when it comes to business networking will you randomly toss out those seeds or will you take your time and cultivate a manageable amount of productive connections? Your choice ... sweet or sour?

$\sim$

66. YOU GET BACK WHAT YOU GIVE

I recently noticed the often used saying "You Get Back What You Give" written in large letters on a roadside display board at a local church. Perhaps they are stating the obvious but then one's base personality of being an optimist or a pessimist might come into play.

Do you see the world as one of opportunity or as one of danger and threats?

If you are a believer in the Law of Attraction you have likely also heard the sayings "you reap what you sew" or "what you think about comes about." Dr. Ivan Misner, Founder of BNI describes this as the "Givers Gain" principal.

The Law of Reciprocity says if you provide a service or favour for another they will likely feel obligated to return the favour. I have read somewhere that it creates a tension in the individual who has received a favour to the extent they feel a discomfort until they have returned the favour and evened the score. This may be at a subconscious level and they wouldn't even be aware of why they are doing it.

The example above refers to the results that can occur for helping another individual. Sometimes, cause and effect aren't related in time. Meaning you can't always see your results nor can they always be attributed to your actions.

The Law of Attraction would have you believe that if you put out something good to the Universe it will respond by having something good return to you. The results you obtain aren't always related to the good you put out though. It could come back to you from a different, perhaps unexpected source.

So what does this have to do with business networking? When you provide assistance or a favour for another individual without the expectation of gain, the Universe will balance it out and you will receive something in return. Providing a business referral to someone in your network could result in multiple referrals back to you.

An easy way to start this in motion is to create and submit a testimonial for someone in your network and submit it to their Linkedin profile under the appropriate heading i.e. where you have worked with them or know of their work.

Odds are they will become motivated to submit one in return on your behalf. This action has an added benefit of displaying your name in their profile which is linked to yours. People are curious and frequently read the Linkedin testimonials. A well written one will reflect well on you.

Another easy favour that you can do for someone is to Like their Facebook page or a specific entry they have made. It helps to give them credibility as well highlights your name somewhat. The same applies to Linkedin. Post a favourable comment on something an individual has written or click on the Like button.

We all have skills and expertise we use everyday in our jobs and businesses. What we take for granted might be awe-inspiring in others. Consider doing some pro bono work for others. Doing so can significantly help someone in need and can also give you that warm fuzzy feeling that we sometimes crave. You never know what you will receive in return once you set this action in place.

If you know the person well enough and you are comfortable doing so, offer their name as a referral if someone is looking for a service or product that they provide.

Whether you believe in the Law of Attraction or not there is enough anecdotal evidence out there that indicates that the principal of "Givers Gain" actually works. I would challenge you to test it out and see for yourself. Try it and see what happens.

Let me know how your net's working.

~

PART IV ADDITIONAL RESOURCES

67. QUESTION: SHOULD YOU SMILE ON YOUR LINKEDIN PROFILE?

Q uestion:

Should you smile on your Linkedin profile?

Answer Provided:

To start with, I'm going to assume you are referring to your Linkedin profile photo.

Smiling is usually good. However, there is a degree of smiling that seems to be generally acceptable.

People do judge a book by its cover as the saying goes. They will make a snap judgement on you based on your headshot photo.

You want to appear to be professional. People usually respond favourably when they see someone smiling. It helps them to warm up to the individual. Smiling seems to help build credibility, at least when they are speaking to a group.

I am led to believe from a Russian colleague that if a fellow Russian was smiling, the automatic response would be "I wonder what they are hiding?"

While smiling would seem appropriate, what about a picture where the individual is laughing? Perhaps if you were in the entertainment industry, it might be appropriate. Not so much I would expect for a Funeral Director or maybe even a Banker.

In a less literal perspective of smiling, I believe our promotional content should be written from a smiling perspective. I have read copy and have said to myself "This person must have been angry when they wrote it."

So, I say, have fun with your Linkedin profile and let your smile shine through your headshot photo and your promotional copy.

~

68. QUESTION: DO YOU ACCEPT CONNECTION INVITATIONS FROM STRANGERS ON LINKEDIN? WHY OR WHY NOT?

Question:

Do you accept connection invitations from strangers on Linkedin? Why or why not?

Answer Provided:

I evaluate every invitation I get to connect. The first criteria I look for is 'do I actually know the person?'

If not, the second criteria is 'are they connected to one of my connections?'

Failing those two, I look to see if we share any common interests.

If they pique my curiosity, I will often connect with them. If I don't see any possible connection or I foresee a barrage of spam from my 'new best friend', I will decline the invite.

I suspect many of the invitations to connect we receive have been instigated by the Linkedin system posting it on the other person's account as someone they might want to connect with.

I often wonder about invites to connect I get from strangers who only have single digit connections and we have nothing in common.

Networking opportunities can certainly be enhanced by leveraging your Linkedin connections however, having potential receptors for any content you are trying to promote through your network can be beneficial.

I've never worried about being watched by 'malicious' people. If they truly are malicious, I have a large enough digital footprint that they could easily find ammo somewhere else besides Linkedin.

~

69. QUESTION: IS NETWORKING MORE IMPORTANT THAN EDUCATION?

Q uestion:

"It's not what you know... it's who you know". Is networking more important than education, as networking saves the long, learning process 'till later?

ANSWER PROVIDED:

I would challenge your opening statement. I don't believe that "It's not what you know. it's who you know" to be true.

I believe "It's not what you know or who you know... but who knows you know!" to be more apt.

From a personal and/or business promotion perspective, it is important to become a content expert i.e. the 'go to person' among your web of connections. You need to tell them what you know. This can be challenging of course. You don't want to come across as being a braggart.

Networking and earning an education are two separate, yet interconnected activities. Both have their merits. One shouldn't be sacrificed at the expense of others.

I don't believe there is evidence supporting your assertion that 'networking saves the long, learning process 'till later?' I think you may actually be referring to the process of mentoring.

An effective mentorship, with somebody who can show you the ropes, so to speak, can speed up the process and help flatten your learning curve.

A mentor can help you with your education. Sage advice can be every bit as important as academic filler.

Networking, on the other hand, can expose you to people who may be able to mentor you in many different areas. It takes cultivating the relationship, bearing in mind the Mentor has to get something out of the relationship from the mentee as well.

～

70. QUESTION: WHAT DO YOU
TALK ABOUT OVER COFFEE?

Q uestion:

What do you talk about over coffee?

When meeting someone for coffee professionally, what do you talk about or try to accomplish? (Particularly if you are in academia and not business)?

Answer Provided:

There is likely a lot less difference between going for coffee whether you are in academia or business, then you think there is. Your approach should be professional in either instance.

Going for coffee is an opportunity to get to know the other person. The objective is to find if you share common interests and if there is any opportunity to collaborate on a project or serve as a resource for each other. If you were in business, it may lead to a joint venture.

Come prepared to talk about subjects that interest you, both in your career and your private life.

I've been on a lot of 'coffee chats.' A lot of business is conducted in local coffee shops in my community.

From my personal experience, plan for 60 minutes for your coffee meeting. I find in that time both of you should have a better understanding of each other. If you resonate with each other, plan for a follow-up coffee meeting.

At the 75 to 90-minute marks, I find the conversation tending to drag and get uncomfortable.

If you want to be considered an exceptional conversationalist, ask meaningful questions of the other person and listen twice as much as you talk. When you give your conversational partner your undivided attention to listening to their favourite topic i.e. themselves, they will think you are a good listener and are likely to be very open to you.

～

71. QUESTION: IN WHAT WAY IS CAREER OR BUSINESS NETWORKING THE SAME AS MAKING GOOD FRIENDS?

Q uestion:

In what way is career or business networking the same as making good friends?

Answer Provided:

I'm going to take a contrary position and say it isn't, in my opinion.

Good friendships develop over time, based on many factors such as trust, reciprocity, longevity, fragility and maintenance.

Where I take exception is the use of the term 'good' when it comes to describing friends.

In our web of connections, we have what can be called our **Crisis Circle**. These are the people we can really count on. You should have at least four people who will be supportive in the event of death, illness, divorce or bankruptcy. They can include family, friends, your doctor or lawyer.

Then there's your **Buddy Circle**. Friends you have fun with, the people who accept you for who you are. There should be at least three people in this circle.

Next, the third circle, is your **Professional Circle.** These are people who know you professionally, can provide reference letters and can speak about the quality of your work and character. You need at least 12 people in this category.

The Fourth Circle is your **Casual Friends Circle.** These are people you share ideas with. You may work with them or know them through organizations or volunteer work. Some may become closer friends and eventually form part of the more inner and intimate circles.

For those of us who have been active on Linkedin, our network of connections would likely fit into the Professional Circle. And many of our Facebook connections would fit into the Fourth Circle of casual friends.

The point I want to make here is as we go through life we connect with countless numbers of people we either maintain contact with or not.

When we network for career or business purposes, it shouldn't be a numbers game. Think quality over quantity. With the right nurturing of the developing relationships, in time, some of these new connections may develop into good friends.

I believe the term 'friends' has been watered down as of late with the terminology becoming ensconced in Facebook practice. Having hundreds or thousands of 'friends' in Facebook does not mean you are well loved or even known for that matter. Try asking some of your distant Facebook friends for a loan of money and see what happens.

When it comes to business and career networking, I think one would be well-advised to consider the possibilities. We will develop strong relationships and some weak ones. Weak ones can be nurtured if there is the possibility of mutual advantage. Perhaps not.

Some will develop into good friends, most won't. Probably the best way to make new friends is to be one yourself.

72. QUESTION: WHAT ARE SOME TIPS WHEN COLLECTING BUSINESS CARDS?

Q uestion:

What are some tips when collecting business cards?

Answer Provided:

First tip... don't collect business cards.

A collection of business cards takes up room and doesn't serve a purpose. Think quality over quantity.

A collection of business cards merely indicates at some point in time, you may or may not have spoken to someone who gave you their business card.

It doesn't necessarily mean you connected with them. If you haven't, I would suspect if you were to contact them a few months past your initial meeting, they may not even remember you.

Your business card is a tool. It is a way to introduce yourself to another individual with the expectation you will mutually decide if you share common interests that may be leveraged into opportunities.

If I collect a business card and I see there is a possibility of an opportunity, I will reach out to the individual. Perhaps it may be sending them some info that may be of interest to them, or perhaps invite them out for coffee.

I will also send them an invitation to connect on Linkedin, explaining where and when we met, in my invitation. Some will accept the invitation, others may not.

If I believe there is value in the connection i.e. that we really did connect, I will add their contact info to my Outlook Contacts for future reference.

~

73. QUESTION: WHAT IS THE MOST DIFFICULT THING ABOUT NETWORKING?

Q uestion:

What is the most difficult thing about networking?

ANSWER PROVIDED:

There likely isn't a definitive answer to this question.

Each and everyone of us is different. While there are difficulties that many networkers face, it isn't universal.

One person may have no problem with walking up to a stranger and introducing themselves, another person may be crippled with fear of having to undertake the same task.

Some people seem to have the gift of the gab. Others are perpetually tongue-tied.

Some can handle their liquor, others can't.

As for me, I have researched the fundamentals of business networking and put them in practice, I still find it difficult to walk up to a group of strangers and insert myself into their conversation. I know <u>how to</u> do it, but would prefer not to.

~

74. QUESTION: WHY IS NETWORKING IMPORTANT IN THE WORKPLACE?

Q uestion:

Why is networking important in the workplace?

Answer Provided:

Is it important? That depends! It may not be important to everybody.

If you are a 'go to work' and 'keep your nose to the grindstone' type of person, it may not be. There are many shy introverts that don't see the value of networking or possess the skills to do so.

Then there are many others who can benefit from networking in the workplace. It can be helpful to be connected to the 'grapevine.' Networking can provide unexpected opportunities.

My professional career is as a Registered Nurse. I work in a small facility and usually work with the same people most of the time. We have worked together for some 15 to 20 years.

I work mostly days on the weekends and nights during the weekdays. I have little exposure to others that work in my system. That doesn't cause me any problems as in my stage of my career, I have little to be gained by networking.

My business life is a completely different story. It is necessary that I network and continue to develop my connections. In the business world its not who you know, but who knows that you know!

My intention is to become the 'go-to-person' when it comes to business networking. It is an ongoing process.

John Jantsch, from Duct Tape Marketing is often quoted as saying "If you aren't networking... you aren't working."

I'm fond of another quote, not sure of where it originated "Networking isn't something you do before work, or after work... it is work!"

~

75. QUESTION: HOW DOES ONE NETWORK EFFECTIVELY WITHOUT SEEMING OR SOUNDING LIKE YOU'RE BRAGGING?

Q uestion:

How does one network effectively without seeming or sounding like you're bragging?

Answer Provided:

If you are bragging when you are networking, you aren't doing it right.

If you are not self-promoting when networking... you aren't doing it right either.

Bragging and self-promoting are not the same thing.

American Cowboy Poet Walt Whitman is quoted as saying 'if you done it, it ain't bragging!'

The main purpose of networking is to expand your sphere of connections with contacts that share mutual interests and can mutually help each other.

To be able to support and refer someone to another, you have to know what they have to offer. They in turn should know what you have to offer.

To be able to learn about common interests, you need to spend some time with another person. Likely there won't be enough time at a networking event, so you need to see about meeting them for a coffee chat.

Back to the effectiveness of networking. One suggestion is that you have your elevator pitch fine-tuned. You need a version to introduce yourself to a group and you need one that is more personal to introduce yourself to one person at a time.

You also need to become skilled at ferreting out those areas of common interest to move the conversation forward quicker.

$\sim$

76. QUESTION: WHO'RE BEST BUSINESS NETWORKING PROFESSIONALS?

Q uestion:

Who're best business networking professionals?

Answer Provided:

Simply answered, the best business networking professionals are those that network professionally.

Being an effective business networker involves quite a few of what might be considered soft skills. Good conversation skills, empathy, listening skills and a genuine interest to help others are a few that readily come to mind.

In attending any business networking event you can expect to see certain professions 'working the room', at least in my experience. Financial planners, realtors and insurance agents readily come to mind.

Some are effective networkers i.e. building contacts and connecting other businesses. Some are like sharks, they expect to make a kill i.e. sale, at the networking event. Those ones give everyone else a bad reputation.

Being a successful business networker involves utilizing strategies that work towards mutual benefits. Sometimes networking is like gardening. You plant seeds. You nurture them. Then with loving care, they grow to fruition.

Networking and building relationships takes time.

~

77. QUESTION: WHAT'S THE BEST WAY TO NETWORK AT 27 WHEN YOU DON'T KNOW MANY PEOPLE AND IT SEEMS LIKE MOST PEOPLE ALREADY HAVE A NETWORK?

Question:

What's the best way to network at 27 when you don't know many people and it seems like most people already have a network?

Answer Provided:

27 or 67, it doesn't really matter, the same principles and strategies apply when it comes to networking.

You ask what the best way to network 'when you don't know many people.' You have identified the gist of the problem i.e. you don't know many people. The short and simplistic answer to would be to get to know more people.

Everybody has to start from somewhere. The purpose of networking is to expand your reach of connections. It's not just a matter of meeting someone and adding them to your list of people you know, it's a matter of connecting with them.

Connecting takes place when you spend some time getting to know the other person, learning what their interests in life are and seeing if you have any common interests. Once you do that, the next step is likely to be of service to your connection. Doing so helps cement the connection.

So how do you get to meet these people? On-line, via social media is one way but the best way is face to face. Belly to belly as some of my business colleagues would say.

I would suggest looking for events in your community that interest you and would likely be attractive to individuals that you want to connect with. Check out http://meetup.com and http://eventbrite.com to see if there are any events in your area that you can attend.

Linkedin is a powerful tool for building your network.

~

78. QUESTION: HOW DO YOU BUILD STRONG RELATIONSHIPS WITH CONTACTS TO STRENGTHEN YOUR NETWORK?

Q uestion:

How do you build strong relationships with contacts to strengthen your network?

Answer Provided:

One of the things I have found when it comes to building and strengthening business relationships is to actively discover the common interests you and the other person have.

Once you discover commonalities you can leverage it for mutual advantage. Note I didn't say 'exploit' for your advantage.

I belonged to a morning breakfast referral networking group. One of their beliefs was people do business with people they like, know and trust. Trust comes from getting to know each other, what the other's business is all about and who would make a good referral for them. They do this by going out for business coffee meetings and getting to know each other.

Spending time with and getting to know your connection is the secret to strengthening the relationship bond.

Some would say 'lead with give, not need." Dr. Ivan Misner Founder of BNI (Business Networking International) takes a little different tact of 'givers gain!'

Both are variations on a theme. When you do something favourable for another person i.e. your connection, a principal called the Law of Reciprocity kicks in.

What happens is that subconsciously the other person feels the need to repay your generosity. They feel the tension until they act upon it. Once they have repaid the perceived debt, they in turn are more likely to want to do something else for you.

You are not really exploiting them in this case either. A general contractor colleague of mine says that he only does business belly to belly. This addresses the earlier statement of doing business with people you know and trust.

～

79. QUESTION: CAN YOU DO TOO MUCH NETWORKING?

Q
uestion:

Can you do too much networking?

Answer Provided:

This question appears to be looking for a definitive answer, where only subjective responses will be provided.

If one defines 'networking' as the face-to-face or on-line interaction with another person, for business purposes and they spend all their time meeting people, at the expense of doing other activities involved in running a business, then perhaps you can do too much networking.

However, if you look at the process of networking as being composed of a series of activities, then perhaps not.

Effective networking is composed of the following activities [and likely even more!]:

· Face to face meeting and interaction

· Researching the other person on-line (before and after meeting them)

· Looking for areas of common interests

· Providing something of value to the other person (product/service) without expectation of receiving something in return

· Keeping up to date with your connection's developments

· Providing public and personal recognition to your connections

· Connecting your connections with other connections for mutual benefits

· Providing referrals to connections that you trust

John Jantsch of Duct Tape Marketing is quoted as saying 'If you're not networking... you're not working!"

Networking needs to be part of your daily activities but not at the expense of running your business.

~

80. QUESTION: ARE MOST BUSINESS PROFESSIONALS GOOD AT NETWORKING?

Q uestion:

Are most business professionals good at networking?

Answer Provided:

This question raises subjective responses.

From my perspective, of those business professionals I know, I would say that they don't.

A comprehensive answer requires exploration of the terms 'good' and 'networking.' And 'business professionals' for that matter.

'Business professionals' isn't a one-size-fits-all category. There are introverts, extroverts, shy people and outgoing ones. The outgoing ones and the extroverts tend to enjoy networking more than the shy and introverted.

But just because a person is outgoing, doesn't necessarily mean they are 'good' at networking. Being a social butterfly or a chatterbox, doesn't necessarily mean you are a good networker.

Effective <u>networking</u> requires strategy i.e. some thought behind what you are doing. It also involves having a purpose and a goal.

As a business professional, networking is a tried and true method of not only increasing your connectedness but your earning potential.

I wasn't a good business networker. I'm not perfect yet but I'm a lot better than many and continually work on improving my effectiveness.

~

81. QUESTION: WHAT ARE YOUR MOST EFFECTIVE CONVERSATION OPENERS IN NETWORKING SITUATIONS?

Question:

What are your most effective conversation openers in networking situations?

Answer Provided:

Effective? The risk is in not coming off like you're using a pick-up line.

I tend to use situational comments.

I'm not averse to using "come here often?" It can elicit a chuckle or two and open the door to conversation.

Others:

"Is this your first time here?"

"Have you ever heard this fellow/woman speak before?"

"I don't think we've ever met. I'm Rae. Ray of sunshine!" also good for a laugh... sometimes.

"Gee, this weather sure sucks!"

I'm not so sure the conversational opener is the most important part.

Perhaps the follow-up question to whatever their response is more important. You would want to go with an open-ended follow-up question to get them talking.

Earlier in this book I described having a Questions Toolbox. The idea is you prepare in advance for questions that can move a conversation forward. It also prepares you for questions you don't want to answer.

Most people like to talk about themselves and their business. And they can easily resonate with you if you are a good listener.

I enjoy a good conversation. Even though my default mode is a shy, introvert, I'm far more outgoing than most people. I find that if I take the lead in the conversation it usually goes well, as I have training in communications.

∾

82. QUESTION: HOW DO I MEET LOCAL PEOPLE WITH COMMON INTERESTS?

Q uestion:

How do I meet local people with common interests?

Answer Provided:

A couple quick suggestions would be to check out Eventbrite & Meetup.

I don't know where you live of course, but both of these, offer access to special interest communities and may very well be local for you.

Another suggestion might be to see if you have any community recreation programs e.g. YMCA/YWCA, as they often have non-academic programs.

I would be remiss if I didn't mention Toastmasters International. Assuming you are over the age of 18, Toastmasters will likely provide everything you are looking for and more! Check out Toastmasters.org.

I have been a member for 25 years so far and it has changed my life for the better.

83. QUESTION: WHAT MAKES A GOOD NETWORKING EVENT?

Q uestion: What makes a good networking event?

That really depends on what benchmarks you use to determine what is good or not.

I have heard of some business people who say if you get more than two free drink tickets with your admission, then it is a good networking event. Some use the food as a measuring stick, assuming there is any food served.

If you are actively looking for prospects, a networking event that provides lots of people to work through i.e. by sheer numbers, a larger event is more likely to be beneficial to you.

If you are an outgoing person and confident in your schmoozing and networking, any size of networking event will probably work for you.

If you are actively looking to expand your connectivity, without regard to amassing prospects, any size of a networking event would work. Chambers of Commerce, business associations, entrepreneur societies, can all be a source of networking opportunities.

Another couple good sources of local networking opportunities are Meetup & Eventbrite. Just search for Business or Networking.

If you are a shy networker, smaller, more organized events may be more to your liking. I don't like the larger events. I don't like being hit on by the sharks who are out to make a quick sale, not into developing a relationship. I have better luck in connecting with smaller networking opportunities.

～

84. QUESTION: WHAT ARE THE BENEFITS OF LIKE-MINDED CONNECTIONS?

Q uestion:

What are the benefits of like-minded connections?

Answer Provided:

IT MIGHT BE HELPFUL TO THINK IN TERMS OF THE MUTUAL BENEFITS OF like-minded connections. While being like-minded, some may call it resonating, certainly makes it easier to communicate your desire to the other person, there is great value in offering something in return.

Being like-minded doesn't mean they are exactly the same as you. We all have our own life-experiences, wants, desires, hopes, prejudices and biases. Even though we are like-minded on specific topics, we are still quite different.

Far too many people in business have the idea they need to get something from somebody, whether at a cost or free. A different approach, as promoted by Dr. Ivan Misner of BNI (Business Networking International) is that of 'givers gain.' The concept simply put, is if you give freely to others, you will receive something of equal or greater value in return.

If you are a Law of Attraction believer the concept is that if you do something favourable for somebody else, without the expectation of return from them, the Universe will see to it you receive something in return. The challenge is in recognizing the fact what you receive in return may not come from the person you gave to. It could come from another source.

In developing an effective business network, like-minded connections compose only one segment for you. Don't rule out connections just because you haven't established commonalities as of yet.

~

85. QUESTION: WHAT RESEARCH EXISTS ABOUT PROFESSIONAL NETWORKING GROUPS?

Q uestion:

What research exists about professional networking groups?

I'm trying to understand the entire market of "professional networking groups" including what are the largest groups, how many people attend, what professions utilize professional networking etc.

Answer Provided:

From my experience, there is very little research, if any on the subject of professional networking groups. Just to clarify the question I would expect you are asking about groups where professionals network, rather than networking groups that are professional in nature. Professional Associations, might meet that criteria.

A couple years ago I decided to research the topic of networking for business purposes. I found there were a few books of value but I didn't really find anything that offered sage advice i.e. from somebody that was speaking to me. My challenges with networking aren't generic, they are specific to me.

In a search of the internet I found literally hundreds of articles on the subject of business networking and since then I have collected hundreds more. In reading these articles a theme became apparent to me. There is a saying in the comedy business, apparently only ever heard by me as nobody else has, that there are only seven original jokes in the world and every joke is actually a version of these seven. We have our knock-knock jokes, which arguably aren't even jokes. We have the traveling salesman. We have two or three people of differing professions walking into a bar... that would hurt! We have puns... the lowest form of humour unless its your own!

I found this to be evident in reviewing the articles. There seem to be a limited number of themes based on the subject of business networking and each writer seemed to be basing their content on what they read in someone else's article. I wasn't seeing anything new or any original ideas.

If I was looking for specific research on the effectiveness of business networking I would check out BNI (Business Networking International). I believe they are the recognized leaders in referral networking groups. Their data may be more anecdotal in nature but I believe there would be value to it.

∾

86. QUESTION: WHAT IS THE BEST WAY TO NETWORK?

Q uestion:

What is the best way to network?

Answer Provided:

I DON'T THINK THERE IS AN ABSOLUTE ANSWER TO THIS QUESTION. THE answer probably lies in one's ability to take advantage of different networking models.

If you are a shy introvert, utilizing the internet in advance to learn more about the people you are going to be networking with, reducing your anxiety and building your self-confidence, then Linked in can be of use.

There is on-line networking and face-to-face networking. While there are many venue types for networking e.g. Chamber of Commerce After Hours, Meetups, BNIs, breakfast networking groups etc., each has its advantages and disadvantages. In most cases they are good for lead generation as in setting up coffee chats with people to get to know them better and explore possible mutual benefits. They are not really designed for doing business or making the sale.

I think the best way to network is to develop a system that works for you, generates good connections/leads and provides a win-win scenario for whoever you are networking with.

～

87. QUESTION: WHAT ARE SOME SPEED NETWORKING TIPS?

Q uestion:

What are some speed networking tips?

Originally asked as...

"What are the speed professional networking tips?"

I'm not sure how to interpret this question. One way would be that the question is looking for tips from professional speed networkers. This would presume that there is a subsector of elite networkers that consider themselves professionals. If so, I would expect that they are self-proclaimed professionals. That leads me to wonder if they are so good, why do they have to keep producing more connections? Wouldn't it be better to build quality relationships with the number of connections they already have i.e. quality over quantity?

Another perspective is that the question is asking for speed networking tips from business professionals that are successful using the format of speed networking. I'll go with the latter.

Speed networking is an organized event where the expectation is that all of the participants will have access to a greater number of personal interactions then they would on their own or at a typical, non-organized meet and greet.

This question is asking for tips i.e. what works and perhaps what doesn't. Here are some to consider based on my experience and opinion.

1. While meeting a large number of people and collecting an equal amount of business cards can look like a measure of success, when it comes to networking and developing relationships, quality is better than quantity. Despite their being a large number of people to meet, you may be more productive with deciding on a number in advance as to how many new people you want to meet. Perhaps 5 to 8 might be a workable number. I find that too high as I tend to forget who was who.

2. In a formalized speed networking event, where you are matched with somebody you already know, there may be advantage to finding more about them and re-establishing your existing relationship.

3. In a less formalized networking event, where you meet someone you already know, there is value in touching base with them. Some so-called networking experts will say that you should never talk to someone you already know as it is a waste of time and they aren't bringing you any new connections and subsequent sales. I totally disagree with that concept. I wouldn't spend a lot of time with a contact or friend but I would touch base to see what is new in their business or personal world and provide them with a brief glance into mine. I would also ask them if they know of anybody at the event I really should meet and if they would be able to introduce me.

4. Be aware of whether the event being billed as a speed networking event actually is one. I am aware of some business association events that while they purport to be a

business event, the members themselves view it as a meat market. No I don't mean 'meet.' Many of the participants are hoping to score at the event.

5. Don't spend too much time with any individual participant. Once the formalities are out of the way don't be afraid of being forward and saying something to the effect of "I think we may have something in common or perhaps we can be of help to each other. Are you interested in going out for coffee to talk some more about it?"

6. Be ready with an exit plan should you meet up with someone who is dominating the conversation or you are receiving bad vibes from. It is a fact of life we will not get along with everyone that we encounter. If you have a sense something is not right, odds are they aren't.

7. Be assertive when it comes to sharing information. "Show me yours and I'll show you mine" comes to mind. If the other person is dominating the conversation either be prepared to steer it in your direction or have an exit strategy.

∾

88. QUESTION: WHAT ARE THE BEST WAYS TO NETWORK AT A BUSINESS DINNER AND LEAVE A GOOD IMPRESSION?

Q uestion:

What are the best ways to network at a business dinner and leave a good impression?

Answer Provided:

Business dinners can be challenging to network at.

There are basically three elements to the event: 1) Pre-meal 2) The meal 3) Post-meal.

1) **Pre-meal:** This is the part where people are coming together. Some are standing around talking to each other, reacquainting themselves with people they already know. It can be challenging to join a group of people if you don't know any of them and introducing yourself to the group. Others may already be sitting at table and talking among themselves. You have the option of sitting at a table of strangers or with people you know. There can be advantages to either option.

You will often find people standing alone. There are shy introverts in every group. They may be waiting for someone to take the initiative to introduce themselves to them. Go for it!

2) **During the meal:** How effective you are in networking here can be limited by how the table is set up. In table rounds of 8 or 10, i.e. standard hotel options, you tend to be limited to the person seated on your right-hand side and/or on your left-hand side. Cross table conversation can be challenging, however group conversations tend to be easier.

If you don't know anybody at the table and/or nobody else has taken the lead, suggest to everybody to go around the table to provide a self-introduction. This is a good opportunity to give an abbreviated elevator pitch and to pass your business cards around the table.

Long, two-sided tables, prevent similar challenges for conversing, in that you are limited to talking to those immediately to your left and your right. As well, depending on the width of the table, to the two or three sitting directly across from you. Once again, your business card and short elevator pitch will be put to use.

3) **Post-meal:** Sometimes people will linger about after the meal which gives you a chance to network. However, more often than naught, people want to get going on their way to other activities. Many may uncomfortable with networking, so don't stick around.

As for the best way to network, basic networking skills come into play. You only have a limited amount of time, so you need to have a plan.

In advance, learn who is attending the event that it would be worth your while to meet. If you see people you know, reacquaint yourself... find out what is new with them. And don't forget to share what is new with you. In addition, when talking to somebody you know, ask them if there is somebody at the event they know, that might be beneficial for you to meet. Then ask them to introduce you.

As in any networking event, you are collecting leads as to possible connections. When talking to someone look for common interests. If so, invite them out for coffee. Get their business card and contact them after the event to confirm the details.

Take advantage of your collection of business cards and send them an invitation to join your professional network on Linkedin.

~

89. QUESTION: HOW DO I NETWORK WITH OTHER PEOPLE IN MY INDUSTRY?

Q uestion:

How do I network with other people in my industry?

Answer Provided:

If I look at your situation strategically, I see several key areas for you to focus on.

Firstly, is the people you work with on a daily basis. Get to know them better. Find out how you can help them. Being of service to another without expectations of something in return can be one of the best ways to grow your network. This includes getting to know your supervisors and managers.

Secondly, expand your circle of contacts. Who are your customers, clients and people you deal with on a regular basis that aren't fellow employees?

Thirdly, is to think of a bigger picture. What industry do you work in? Do they have professional development or training opportunities? This can put you in contact with people in the same industry, yet working for a different company.

Does your industry have an Association? Associations often have annual or more often meetings where you can attend and get a larger and more diverse group of potential contacts.

～

90. QUESTION: HOW DO I GET BETTER AT NETWORKING IN CONFERENCES AND EVENTS?

Q uestion:

How do I get better at networking in conferences and events?

Answer Provided:

At the risk of starting off by stating the obvious, to get better at networking at conferences and events you have to actually attend them.

And then it isn't a matter of attending any conference or event. There needs to be a purpose to attending. What is your goal? What do you hope to achieve?

In my book **Power Networking for Shy People: Tips & Techniques for Moving from Shy to Sly!** I outlined a series of steps that a networker can take to be a more effective networker.

Strategies include researching the event on-line. Learn all you can about the organization and what they are all about. Who are the leaders or the people of influence? What type of people go to their events and could there be anyone that would be worth your while meeting?

It isn't a matter of going in for the sale. It is more important to build relationships. You won't build the relationship at the event. You need to follow-up after the event. Invite your new connection out for coffee. Get to know them!

While it is great to meet and listen to other people's stories, you have to be prepared to promote yourself. This is where your elevator pitch and your USP [Universal Sales Proposition] comes into play. What makes you different from everybody else?

You only improve your skills by practicing them. After a networking event, debrief yourself. What worked? What didn't? What will you do differently next time?

$\sim$

91. QUESTION: WHY ON LINKEDIN HAS BOASTING ABOUT ONESELF AND ONE'S ACHIEVEMENTS BECOME ACCEPTABLE AND APPLAUDED? DOES BRAGGING OR HUMILITY SERVE SOCIETY BETTER?

Question:

Why on LinkedIn has boasting about oneself and one's achievements become acceptable and applauded? Does bragging or humility serve society better?

Answer Provided:

You ask two separate questions. Addressing the first one "Why on LinkedIn has boasting about oneself and one's achievements become acceptable and applauded?"

I'll break my response further down. You are asserting people are 'boasting' about themselves. I don't necessarily agree with that statement.

Sure, with the sheer numbers of Linkedin members, there would have to be those who are boasting about their accomplishments. They likely do it in other aspects of their lives, be it on-line, or in person.

Linkedin has developed into a platform that allows the member to 'market' themselves.

I find many people have a challenge with the concept of self-promotion. My perspective is North American. I realize different cultures may have different views on self-promotion or talking about one's accomplishments.

I'm fond of a quote from Walt Whitman, American Cowboy Poet. He said that 'if you have done it... it ain't bragging!"

Creating promotional copy in your Linkedin profile that promotes you as a solution to somebody else's problem takes skill. You want to get the message across, featuring your skills, without coming across as bragging/boasting. This can be challenging if you have a lot of things on the go and desirable skills.

Is it becoming acceptable and applauded? It would answer that question by saying it has become expected and an effective tool for promoting one's self.

If a person is searching for work, they would be well-advised to have an effective Linkedin profile that resonates with their resume. You can almost guarantee that an employer will take a look at your Linkedin profile before inviting you in for an interview, as part of their screening process.

I'm not so sure about the applauded part of the question. If your Linkedin profile doesn't reveal much about you, your requests for invitations to connect might be on the lean side.

I personally don't connect with Linkedin invitations who don't have a headshot photo, don't have any information about themselves or LIONS (Linkedin Open Networkers).

You ask '**Does bragging or humility serve society better?**'

Personally, I don't think either does. But then again, why should it require an either/or response?

I believe that there is an appropriate time to promote yourself and there are times humility is more appropriate.

I find inspiration in 'everyday heroes.' These are people who have undertaken acts of bravery or courageous ones and when asked about it, reply with something like "I just did what needed to be done."

~

92. QUESTION: WHAT ARE TIPS AND TRICKS TO INCREASE YOUR ODDS OF GETTING A JOB AT A COMPANY BY USING NETWORKING SKILLS?

Q uestion:

What are tips and tricks to increase your odds of getting a job at a company by using networking skills?

Answer Provided:

I would suggest utilizing a multi-faceted approach.

Firstly, research the company on-line. Locate and read their social media properties. More than likely they will have a Facebook business page, a Linkedin Business page and possibly a Twitter profile.

Find out what is important to the company. What do they believe in? What is important to them? What are they most proud of?

Secondly, find out who the key people behind the company are. What roles do they take on in the company? Then check out their individual profiles on Linkedin.

If you are comfortable in doing so, send them an invitation to connect on Linkedin and provide them with a reason they might want to connect. Not the fact you are looking for a job though.

If the company's social media properties allow for posting comments, see how you can add value by posting replies to their postings.

Networking face-to-face with people in hiring positions in companies can be tricky, in that in most cases, their networking is restricted to events with other members of the company.

There can be benefit in leveraging your connections to see if anybody knows anyone working at the company in question, or if they have any connections there.

If you are gutsy, you may want to contact somebody in the company for an informational chat, where you ask for the opportunity to pick their brain.

In business networking events, it can be helpful to ask people you connect with out right "Do you know anybody that works at...?

I go into strategies such as these in greater detail in my book **You're Hired! Job Search Strategies That Work.**

$\sim$

93. QUESTION: WHICH TOOLS OR APPS DO YOU USE TO NETWORK EFFECTIVELY AT EVENTS?

Question:

Which tools or apps do you use to network effectively at events?

Answer Provided:

I'm not a person who would put the words 'tools or apps' in the same sentence as "networking effectively."

Networking effectively is belly to belly, face to face. Forget the electronic gadgets.

Talk to people. Get to know them. Allow them to get to know you. Build relationships.

Use the gadgetry before an event to research people that it could be advantageous to meet at the event. Linkedin is good for that.

Follow-up with people you meet at an event via phone call or e-mail. Sending an invitation to connect via Linkedin can be helpful.

∾

94. QUESTION: WHAT ARE THE CHALLENGES OF WRITING A LINKEDIN PROFILE?

Q uestion:

What are the challenges of writing a Linkedin profile?

Answer Provided:

The question asks what are the <u>challenges </u>of writing a Linkedin profile.

Challenges are relative to the person creating their own Linkedin profile.

It may depend on several factors:

You need to have a high level of literacy. Any spelling mistakes or grammatical errors you make will work against you.

You need to have good strategic thinking skills. We all likely have a long list of jobs, skills and/or accomplishments we could post. But should we? Your Linkedin profile has to be consistent with your purpose of creating it in the first place. Sometimes, less is more.

You need to get comfortable with promoting yourself. As a business would when marketing itself, your Linkedin profile is marketing you.

You need to make sure it is written to present you in the best possible light.

It's no longer a matter of sharing what you have done in the past, it's a matter of promoting what you can do in the future. You need to craft your content so it comes across as a solution to somebody else's problem.

You need to get comfortable with writing about yourself in the 3rd person vs 1st person 'I' statements.

If you are searching for work, your Linkedin profile has to be consistent with your resume. Your Linkedin profile allows you to expand upon some of the claims you have made on your resume and provide examples of your work.

You need to fill out all of the areas in your profile. This not only means filling in dates and titles, it means providing content that once again, shows you in a good light.

You need to actively build your network of connections. Consider 500 connections as a minimum. It may be the first thing many people look at. If your connections number is low, some may wonder if it's worthwhile connecting to you.

Linkedin is one of many social media venues. You need to ensure your digital footprint is consistent with the professional image you want to portray.

You should consider your Linkedin profile as being iterative. It needs to be tweaked and adapted on an ongoing basis.

If you are using it for job searching, you may want to keep a file of different content e.g. jobs and duties you have had in the past and then change your Linkedin profile whenever you are applying for a job.

From my perspective, there are at least two categories of connections on Linkedin. There are those that take a lackadaisical approach to connecting and those who take it very seriously.

Linkedin is merely a tool for you to use to promote yourself. At present, it is likely the best one for achieving results.

$\sim$

95. NOW WHAT?

At times like this I am reminded by the mosquito in a nudist camp quote... "I know what to do but I don't know where to start!"

You didn't become shy overnight so odds are it will take you a while to become a confident networker.

It can be overwhelming to think about what you need to do. Hopefully, this book has helped you to develop an approach to dealing with your shyness and anxiety in your networking activities. I know that it has worked for me.

I am fond of the saying "How do you eat an elephant?" The answer being... "one bite at a time!"

My suggestion would be to pick away at the pieces of the approach outlined in this book and try incorporating them one at a time. Test them out. See how they work. See what doesn't work. Working with a buddy can be very helpful.

Feel free to share your success stories with me and perhaps your <u>not so successful</u> stories. I can be reached at shynomore@powernetworkingforshypeople.com.

ABOUT THE AUTHOR

Rae A. Stonehouse is a Canadian born author & speaker.

His professional career as a Registered Nurse working predominantly in psychiatry/mental health, has spanned four decades.

Rae has embraced the principal of CANI (Constant and Never-ending Improvement) as promoted by thought leaders such as Tony Robbins and brings that philosophy to each of his publications and presentations.

Rae has dedicated the latter segment of his journey through life to overcoming his personal inhibitions. As a 25+ year member of Toast-masters International he has systematically built his self-confidence and communicating ability. He is passionate about sharing his lessons with his readers and listeners.

His publications thus far are of the self-help, self-improvement genre and systematically offer valuable sage advice on a specific topic.

His writing style can be described as being conversational. As an author, Rae strives to have a one-to-one conversation with each of his readers, very much like having your own personal self-development coach.

Rae is known for having a wry sense of humour that features in his publications. To learn more about Rae A. Stonehouse, visit the Wonderful World of Rae Stonehouse at http://raestonehouse.com.

ALSO BY RAE A. STONEHOUSE

PROtect Yourself! Empowering Tips & Techniques for Personal Safety: A Practical Violence Prevention Manual for Healthcare Workers https://books2read.com/protectyourself

∾

E=Emcee Squared: Tips & Techniques to Becoming a Dynamic Master of Ceremonies

https://books2read.com/emceesquared

∾

Power of Promotion: On-line Marketing for Toastmasters Club Growth

https://books2read.com/powerofpromotion

∾

You're Hired! Job Search Strategies That Work (This is the complete program)

E-book & Paperback: https://books2read.com/yourehired

On-line E-course: (Available as a self-directed or instructor-led program) http://liveforexcellenceacademy.com/

∾

You're Hired! Resume Tactics: Job Search Strategies That Work

E-book & Paperback: https://books2read.com/resumetactics

On-line E-course: http://liveforexcellenceacademy.com/

～

Job Interview Preparation: Job Search Strategies That Work

E-book & Paperback: https://books2read.com/jobinterviewpreparation

On-line E-course: http://liveforexcellenceacademy.com/

～

You're Hired! Leveraging Your Network: Job Search Strategies That Work

E-book & Paperback: https://books2read.com/leveragingyournetwork

On-line E-course: http://liveforexcellenceacademy.com/

～

You're Hired! Power Tactics: Job Search Strategies That Work (This is a box set containing the complete content of Resume Tactics, Job Interview Preparation & Leveraging Your Network)

E-book: https://books2read.com/powertactics

～

If you have found this book and program to be helpful, please leave us a warm review wherever you purchased this book.

www.ingramcontent.com/pod-product-compliance
Lightning Source LLC
Chambersburg PA
CBHW071326210326
41597CB00015B/1369